Beyond the Mirror

Ashley Weis

WINSLET PRESS

Beyond the Mirror
Copyright © 2011 by Ashley Weis

To learn more visit:
www.morethandesire.com

All rights reserved. No portion of this book may be reproduced, stored in a retrieval system, or transmitted in any form or bay any means—electronic, mechanical, photocopy, recording, scanning, etc.—except for quotations in reviews or articles, without the prior written permission of the publisher.

Library of Congress Control Number: 2011924212

ISBN-10: 0615458238
ISBN-13: 978-0615458236

All scripture is taken from the New King James Bible.

Cover & Interior Design by George Weis of Tekeme Studios

Printed in the United States of America

First Edition: March 2011
11 10 9 8 7 6 5 4 3 2 1

To any woman who has ever been burned by the lie that she's not good enough, this is for you.

"...Christ in you, the hope of glory."
Colossians 1:27

# Table of Contents

Dear Wife

Marriage in Full View

Our Marriage is Dead	7
Marriage is Worth Fighting For	9
If He's Fighting, But Still Falling	13
One Day the Pain Will Lessen	17
Making Your Husband an Idol	19

Reflection of Your Heart

Just the Way You Are	25
An Ugly Wife	31
Sensitive to Lust, Not Insecurity	35
Self-Insecurity vs. Husband-Insecurity	39
God's Beautiful Garden	43
What Is Insecurity?	45
How to Kill Insecurity	47
Your Damaged Heart	49
Your Beauty Defined	53

Behind the Lies

MASK #1 - Appearance to the World	61
MASK #2 - False Humility & Self-Pity	67
MASK #3 - Busy Little Bees	71
MASK #4 - Judgment & Comparison	75
MASK #5 - Appearance to Self	79

# Table of Contents

Shattering the Delusion

Appearance to God	85
Pure in Heart	91
The Stages of Sin	99
Fighting Temptations	105

The Son in Your Eyes

Jesus is Better than Vodka	111
All for Him	113
Before the Throne	115
It's Not About Me	117
Be Your Own God	119
Love Letters to Jesus	123

Heart to Heart

Does it Ever Get Better?	133
Love Can Overcome This	143
Our New Beginning	173

Dear Wife

Healing after I found porn on my husband's computer, honestly, was one of the hardest things I've ever endured. Everything you are feeling right now and everything you felt when you found out, I felt.

My husband George stopped looking at porn, but I still couldn't trust him. When he left the house alone, I felt like my lungs caved in and twisted around my heart. Every moment he was gone I imagined the worst scenarios. Gorgeous, immodest girls walking around. His eyes taking in every detail of their bodies. His heart beating, wondering if he'd have more fun with a girl like that—a girl so different from me.

I knew George loved me. He didn't love the women he looked at. They were in his fantasyland—separate from me. But I wanted to be enough for my husband. I hated that he needed a fantasy world where women looked and did everything he wanted—everything I didn't do. I wanted to captivate him. I still want this. I want both his eyes and heart. I want to be enough. And I know you want the same.

Please know that I am with you. I have been where you are. The pain and anger, all of the tears soaked into your pillow, the nights you're too numb to cry—I know. And many other women know what it feels like to be crushed by their husband's sexual sin, too. We know what it's like to feel like we'll never measure up. And we're not alone. We're in this together.

Sometimes people tell us to get over it or get used to it. All men look. All men fantasize. As long as they come home to us, that's all that matters. But this is so far from real love and pure desire—and it's certainly not romantic.

Beyond the Mirror

I don't know about you, but my wedding vows meant the world to me. When I realized my husband hid his affair with porn, those vows felt like lies. Everything did. It's heartbreaking to fall in love, be broken to pieces, and then wonder if your love was ever real to begin with.

The love and romance in the beginning. The wedding vows. Was it all fake? Was he looking at porn the night before we got married? Thoughts like this will come and go, still, but don't dwell on them anymore.

Let's grow together. Let's surpass these negative thoughts and feelings and let God transform our hearts. My life's motto is *Beauty after Rain*. One of the reasons I picked that motto is because my most meaningful times in life, my deepest joys, have come after the most painful circumstances. God carves us, shapes us, and in the process we get cut by the sharpest blades.

George's lies and lust sliced open wounds that already existed. He went deeper than anyone ever did. I remember crying in bed one night as George slept beside me. The only thing that ran through my head, over and over, was, "He ruined me."

But porn didn't ruin me. It didn't ruin our marriage. I chose to stand up to the lies and say, "My marriage is worth fighting for."

It's been a difficult fight. A painful, bloody, but hopeful fight. But if there is one thing I know to be true, it's that the devil hates marriage. And I wasn't about to let him have his way.

My hope within the pages of this book is that your smile will be genuine and your joy will be complete. That you will find a little glimmer of hope by hearing my story and learning how to look "beyond the mirror."

I want you to feel what I feel. To know that you can overcome this. Your heart can heal. And you can be content in who God made you to be. You can discover the growth and beauty that comes after the rain.

If I were writing this on paper you would see splotches of smeared ink where my tears have landed. No, that's not me trying to be poetic. It's true. I know the immense pain you are going through. I know what it's like to feel like you're not enough, to cry so hard you can't breathe. I know what it's like to feel numb, like death would be so much better than being married

Looking Inward

to him. I know. I have felt everything you are feeling now. But listen to me: your heart is precious. So is mine. Through all of this I almost forgot that. But now I know. And I want you to know, too.

YOU are worth fighting for.

If you need someone to talk to feel free to email me. When I went through this I didn't have ANYONE to talk to about it. No one felt my pain. I feel your pain. And I'm here.

Hang in there,

Ashley (ashley@morethandesire.com)

Marriage in Full View

Our Marriage is Dead

I'll never forget the weekend my wedding rings sat on the ledge in the kitchen. I took them off during a horrible fight where many, many curses came from my mouth. George slept in the living room that night and I slept alone, weeping in our bedroom. Our bedroom. Ours. I still wanted to be *us*, but it never felt like he was fighting hard enough. I was in so much pain and working so hard to trust him again, but it seemed like he never told me the things I wanted him to tell me.

He feared my reaction. I feared his actions. We went through cycle after cycle of fearing each other and ended up sleeping alone with my wedding rings far from my finger, too far from my heart. Our marriage died.

A friend of mine who is going through this told me a few nights ago, "Our marriage is dead. It's over. We're done."

I took her words seriously, but also knew they were only part true. Yes, their marriage has died, but it's not over. Death never means the end. It feels unnatural to die, but death brings light and resurrection.

Our marriage died and I can't tell you how thankful I am for its death. We had a good marriage, even through lust. It was painful, but we still had good memories sprinkled throughout. The bad did not make the good mean any less (although I thought so at times). The good was still real. But without the death of our self-centered marriage we wouldn't have made it through the fire. We were on two different paths headed to different destinations. Now, we're on the same path. Resurrected. New. Complete. We fight for each other and with each other. We sometimes disagree and get annoyed, but we don't fight. We know that it's better to serve the other than to be served. We are willing to do whatever it takes to make the other person happy, even if it means being uncomfortable ourselves.

There is beauty in death. Close your eyes. Let your current painful marriage die. Pile the dirt on it and walk away, remembering the good and bad but preparing yourself for something better. Then, open your eyes and discover the beauty of a resurrected marriage. And fight, every day of your life, to keep your new marriage alive.

Marriage is Worth Fighting For

One year after I first found out about George's porn addiction I sank to the floor in my baby's bedroom. With her in my arms, I thought about leaving. I stood, put her on my hip, and looked at our car through my tears. *I could just leave now and he'd never know.*

I looked into my baby's eyes, back to the car, back to her eyes, and cried hysterically. Why? Because I knew I couldn't leave. I loved him. Oh, I hated it. I hated that I loved him. I wanted to leave. I wanted to get rid of the pain and I thought that would be the only way how. I didn't believe him a year after he stopped looking at women lustfully ... how could I ever? Our marriage was a lie. Where romance once breathed our love burned in lies and bitterness. I wanted to leave. I wanted to show him how it felt to be betrayed. I just wanted to be done. The pain. The ache in my chest. The extreme battle with insecurities that I believed he caused. I needed it to be over.

But I couldn't.

I loved him.

No matter how bad a marriage gets, no matter how many times our spouses cheat on us, there are always, underneath the mess, wedding vows that were once true. We said them with love in our eyes. Remember that feeling when you were pronounced husband and wife? Wow. There's no feeling like that. And underneath every dying marriage, those vows and those feelings still exist.

Many people treat marriage as though it's nothing more than a pet. Get a spouse because they're cute and make you feel good, get rid of them when

Beyond the Mirror

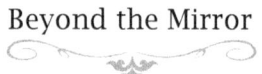

they annoy you, and get a new one so you can feel good again. Repeat and repeat and repeat until you end up lonely, wondering why your relationships never work out.

Living in truth, being a beautiful spouse, means living in God's love and knowing that marriage is worth fighting for. That means this: You do whatever (w-h-a-t-e-v-e-r) it takes to make it work. You stop looking for reasons to end it, like I did back then. And you replace those negative thoughts with positive ones. For every negative thought you have of your spouse, you think of three positive until you can no longer think negatively of him/her. You stop looking for reasons to leave and look for reasons to stay. You change your focus from yourself and your own desires, to the desires of your spouse. If both people do this a marriage will not only survive, but thrive. If one person does this and the other doesn't a marriage can survive, but may also die. If both people choose themselves over the other person ... well, welcome the death of your marriage.

Sacrificial love changes lives. It's not easy amidst the brokenness betrayal brings. But I know it's possible. I know it is because God illustrates this time and time again. Look at Hosea, staying faithful to Gomer no matter what. Look at God ... just look at what He does for you and how little you do for Him.

Look at us. George and me. I wanted to leave him, to cheat on him, to kill his heart with my words for what he did to me. There were times I genuinely believed I hated him. Times I couldn't remember why I married him. Times I would have rather been single my entire life (so I thought) than be married to him.

Look at us now. There isn't a day that passes where we don't kiss. He still holds my hands. We long for each other amidst our hectic lifestyle with kids. We help each other. We give to each other when we feel like we have nothing to give. We talk about porn pretty much daily and the word no longer makes us shiver, it makes us ache for people like you. People who can relate to what we went through but haven't seen the other side yet.

We want that for you. If our marriage could survive the flames ... yours

can too. But to live in truth, to see your marriage renewed, you have to lay your lives down for each other. I can't stress this enough. And it's not easy. It causes both people to look at their own flaws, be truly sorrowful for their actions, and allow God to change their hearts. I think allowing God to change us is the most difficult part. It's one thing to say, "I'm sorry for hurting you last night." It's an entirely different story to say, "God, have your way with me," when we want to have our own way, just like Burger King tells us.

There is an easy way to live. A way so common to Burger King and the world. But it's not worth much in the sight of heaven. The difficult way, the narrow way, it leads to life. The eternal life of your soul and the life of your relationships. And if there is one thing I know … it's that your soul (and your marriage) are worth fighting for. The narrow way, while more difficult on earth, is worth it.

If He's Fighting, But Still Falling

Yes, he cheated. He may continue to cheat by continuing to struggle with this. But my question is this ... is it a battle for him? Does he desire to change, but just can't get there yet? Or is he sitting around looking at porn and telling you that you need to deal with it because that's just how he is?

If it's a battle for him, then you have to realize that he doesn't love lust more than you. If he did it wouldn't be a battle. Instead, it would be part of the "package" to be married to him. Some men are like that. Some men look at other women, see no problem with it, and expect their wives to deal with it or leave. They don't care about the hearts of their wives or their own hearts—they just want to have fun, live life with "no consequences," and pretend that everything is okay ... when in reality their spirits are rotting.

If your husband is in a battle, then he is not only in this battle for himself, but for you. What you have to realize is that lust is one of the absolute worst addictions out there. Unlike alcohol, it's readily available and free. It's not easy to stop these patterns for a man. We wish they could. We wish there would be no battle, that our husbands would see our pain and never look at another woman again. That's not the case. There is a battle and if both people want their marriage to triumph they must be willing to fight every day of their lives ... forever.

Remember, also, that your faithfulness does not depend on his faithfulness. Your love does not depend on his love for you. And remember that he does love you, it's just hard for you to understand the grip lust has on men. It's not what women often think it is. It's literally like a drug. And it's so, so hard for men to stay pure in this world. Think about it ... women often wear tight skirts and jeans to church. Young girls wear even more immodest clothing. Nothing is hidden anymore. Commercials are filled with sensuality. Most people love *The Notebook*, a movie I despise.

Know why despise it? Sensuality is all over the place in that movie. There may not be full-blown porn stuff happening, but there's enough to make it inappropriate. Also, the woman character in the movie is engaged when she comes back to have sex with her "soul-mate." Not only is that a horribly unromantic thought to me, but I think the camera shows a little too much in that scene of passionate unfaithfulness.

How many movies out right now are appropriate sensuality-wise? Not many. But a major percentage of couples watch them anyway, thinking nothing of the sensuality drawn before them.

If a husband is serious about this battle … he needs to cut out his eye. Movies like *The Notebook* really need to lose their appeal. We don't need to watch two people have sex on a screen whether there is nudity or not. It's inappropriate. There is nothing pure and lovely about *The Notebook*, save the faithfulness he portrays as an old man. And who knows … it's Hollywood. They only give us the "good parts." They don't tell us if he looked at other women when his wife had trouble remembering him.

We live in reality here. Those movies corrupt our view of purity just as much as porn. George did love me when he betrayed me by looking at porn. Lust is betrayal, but it's a lot different than divorcing me and never talking to me again. Men are trained to lust in this world just as much as women are trained to want to be enough. It's a great cycle for the devil. And often women buy into it by watching things like *The Notebook* with their husbands, yet expecting them to not have impure thoughts.

We must fill our lives with all that is pure and purge the negative influences around us. Both man and woman must do this. Marriages can be okay without true purity and intimacy—they may even have romance. But they are not as wonderful as they could be. If your husband is in a battle and not just telling you to deal with the way he is … then trust that he loves you. Help each other find ways to overcome this. Talk about what you can cut out of your life that is a negative influence and ask God to show you what you can do to support him.

Remember, this is bigger than we realize. As women we often think we are the only victim. What we don't realize is that our husband's are in just as much pain as we are, they just don't realize it like we do. That's how crafty the devil is. Porn stars, women who dress immodestly—every soul affected by lust is a hurting soul. But God is here to heal us, to bring us into a hope-filled and beautiful marriage that is better than we ever imagined.

If he's fighting, but falling ... trust that he loves you. There are just too many arrows coming at him and he doesn't know how to dodge them and fully fight in this battle yet. Learn with each other. Grow with each other. And fight with each other with all you have.

One Day the Pain Will Lessen

A few years back George was at work. He had already shown me that he was a changed man, but I refused to let my heart feel what my mind knew. When he went to work I'd cry and cry and cry. Through those tears I'd get angry and call him (or write in my journal), "How could you do this to us?" Just how could he have risked our marriage for pornography, for the beauty of other women? What about me? Why did he marry me?

Oh, so many of these thoughts entered my mind and dwelt there. I cried out to God, "Will the pain ever go away? It seems to get worse every day. It's not fair that he's getting better and I'm getting worse."

I honestly believed I'd always be suffering. I mean, he worked outside of the home, he had to go out in public, he'd see people for the rest of his life, and his job is web design, that means pretty pictures of models a lot of the time.

Somewhere along the journey my pain started to lift. Little by little the truth sunk into my heart. And it dwelt there, pushing all the negative thoughts away. Every now and then there's still a thought, "What if he does it again?"

Before, I'd give into that thought with, "Yes, what if he does? How will I get through that? It would be unbearable. I would distance myself from him and never allow him back into my heart."

This thought pattern would make me suspicious, jealous, and insecure even when I had nothing to feel this way about.

Now, I combat that thought with, "That's between him and God. I hope he seeks purity and God and turns from the world." Then, I pray for

Beyond the Mirror

his purity. I no longer ask him, "Hey, how's the lust thing going?" Because I don't want to dwell in the sin. Instead, I try to talk about God as much as possible. In some marriages, this isn't possible. Your husband rejects God. But remember, that's what he is doing. He is rejecting God and in turn rejecting you. It's not just about you.

You can still heal from this, no matter how little your husband changes. Your pain WILL lessen one day if you allow it to. For me, I had to stop allowing negative thought patterns to take over my life. I had to stop dwelling in my husband's sin (and my own) and seek the purity and holiness of God. The suffering lessens when we see the suffering as a gift, because we know that it brings us closer to God. It makes us more like Him. To live life with joy because everything goes your way and everyone loves you is easy. But to live life with joy because you love God and are willing to suffer for His sake and the sake of others … that isn't easy. But it is ten times more beautiful.

True joy doesn't come with a painted on smile. But it does come with peace in the midst of a storm. True joy will lessen your pain. It will offer you a hand and calm the sea. You won't drown in this pain. Take the hand of Christ, cling to Him, and set your mind on things above. He won't let you down.

Making Your Husband an Idol

Part of the reason George's porn struggle broke me so much was because I placed him above God in my life. We had an extremely close relationship. We were always together. And he was everything I ever wanted. It was impossible not to be obsessed at that point. But in our whirlwind romance we both put God on the back burner and in my own heart George almost became a god to me.

Because of this ... I felt like my entire essence was shattered when I unraveled all of the details of his struggle with lust. My entire life felt meaningless. My beauty ... non-existent. He affirmed something I felt for years and years before him: *I am not enough. I never will be.*

See, when I met George he swept me off my feet, my prince charming. He rescued me from all of the insecurities I lived with for so long. He made me feel like enough. My beauty, finally, found the validation it yearned for. I felt perfect. Life made sense and I had the romance I searched for all those years.

But I was wrong. I gave George too much power over my heart. I treated him as though he were God, able to validate me and never let me down. I only have one true Prince Charming, and it's not my husband. Yes, my husband completes me. He is still my prince charming on this earth, but he is not someone who can validate my worth as a human. He is not perfect, he is not God, and I can't expect him to be.

But I did.

I expected him to never hurt me, to always love me more than himself, and to have eyes only for me. I made him an idol and cared less and less about what God thought of me. When his porn struggle came to the surface my heart immediately went into a frenzy. I wanted to change anything I could about myself so I could be the most beautiful woman in the world to my husband. I yearned for changes in my physical body so that I would be the only woman my husband ever found attractive (a joke, right?). And it killed me. I stopped caring about God's view of me and desperately longed for the validation of this world and my husband.

There is a certain "validation" a husband can give. He can love me more than himself (which he does now). He can make me feel beautiful and loved. He can live his life in such a way that I know without a doubt that although I am flawed and although there are other attractive women in the world ... my husband chooses me and only me with all of this heart.

But my worth, my beauty—that is not something I can expect my husband to validate. I don't even think we (as humans) fully comprehend the depth and glory of true beauty. If we try to see ourselves and others through our own eyes, through the world's eyes, or through any lens other than God's ... we're going to see a tainted beauty.

It wasn't until I took my husband out of God's place in my life and gave God the place He deserves (first place) that I truly began to change. My insecurities didn't begin to heal until I learned what it means to love myself through God's heart. We can focus on the beauty of this world, a beauty that is often tainted with sensuality or sex, and we will become less and less beautiful in reality. We can focus on pleasing our husband's lustful eye, or comparing ourselves to other women, or never being content with our natural, no make-upped, childbirth scarred bodies ... and we will miss true beauty.

True beauty isn't just spiritual. It's physical, too. It radiates from the inside out. It's more than just a bright smile, it's a smile filled with confidence in God's love. It's a smile that knows it doesn't have to compete with the world or get attention from the world in order to feel like enough.

The world will always let us down. Our husbands, if given the place of God, will let us down. It's inevitable. No one can make us feel like

enough. And guess what? God doesn't even ask us to be enough. Through His beautiful grace we know that there is no enough. There is no end to our growth or beauty. It transcends time. It transcends everything this world knows. It lives and breathes after our earthly bodies are placed six feet under.

We should never strive for an end, an enough, a feeling of being there, being it, because it will never happen. We should strive to love God more, to know Him more, and to cling to Him so much more than we do now. Through that … we will understand what it means to rest in who we are and to grow without desiring to be enough. We will understand that the world will never think we are enough and that we no longer want or need that from the world.

Your beauty will never be enough to this world, because true beauty is too much for this world.

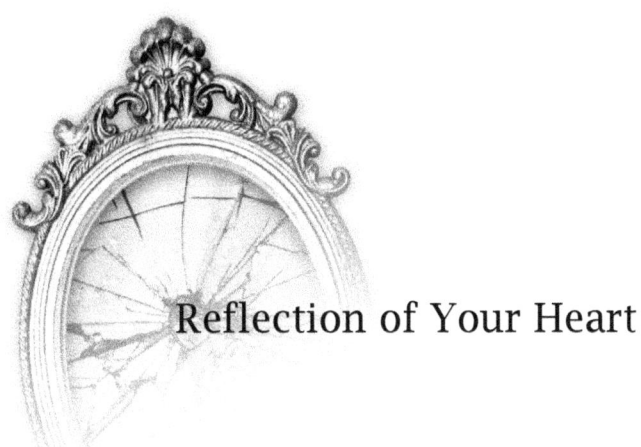

Reflection of Your Heart

Just the Way You Are

There is a survey on our website for women who have gone through the devastation of discovering their husband's porn addictions. One thing that has stood out to me recently is the fact that most women rate themselves below 6. A lot of women rate themselves below 4. And only one woman who took this survey rated herself a 10. About half of these women said God would rate them below a 10 as well.

The survey also asks women to rate their favorite woman celebrity on a scale from 1-10. Most say between 8-10. This saddens me. Especially when I read the reasons why women are not rating themselves with a 10.

Here are some of the reasons:
- Mom to 5 sons with birth flaws, aging 44-year-old body, breasts that nursed all my babies. Recent weight loss that helped in skin sagging. God is disappointed in how I see myself.
- I do not measure up to the physical ideal of my husband.
- I have lost much of my hair and am overweight. Though I try to "pretty" myself for my man by staying out of sweats and caring about my appearance, there is only so far 'cleanliness' can go. That said, he tells me often, "I wish you could see yourself the way that I see you…" – So do I.
- I know that I fall far short of what anyone would rate a ten.

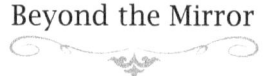

  I doubt that God could think that, I know He made me uniquely me and He finds that beautiful. But God would not be delusional and rate me a 10.
- Because I'm fat.
- I don't think I'm pretty according to the world's standards. I think God would like to see me take better care of my body—exercise and eat better.
- Because I feel there are many more women who are more beautiful than I am. I am very attractive, but there are many who are more attractive if you measure the way most of society does. I didn't rate a 10 in God's eyes because I could take better care of myself.

CUT OUT YOUR OWN EYE

I want to address a few of these reasons, as they break my heart to pieces. First of all, stop submerging yourself in this culture. We all know that this culture tries to make women feel insecure. They want us to buy their products, so they make us feel like we need them in order to be beautiful.

We already know that. Enough of it. Get rid of the TV. Get rid of the magazines. We don't need negativity spinning in our hearts. And we can argue that physical beauty is not important, that it's only the inner self that matters, but that's not true. Do you think God wasted His time designing you? Do you think He makes things that are not beautiful? It's all in our perspectives. And our perspectives are often way off target.

TRUE PERSPECTIVE OF BEAUTY

There are plenty of animals, plants, and even people in this world that many of us would consider "ugly" or "unattractive." But that doesn't mean they actually are. It just means we have a distorted view of beauty. We have a view of beauty that is molded by the world, instead of God. He is the Creator of everything, even the things we call ugly or "not as pretty as that one." He

created skin to stretch and sag from childbirth. He could have made it go back to normal without doing this, but He chose not to. Maybe He sees beauty in things we don't. Maybe He isn't concerned about a flat stomach with no marks. Maybe He's more concerned about the child that created those marks.

We don't see things through His eyes enough. We're too immersed in the world. We see things the way the world wants us to see them. We see ourselves as lacking, never enough, and beauty is something we feel we will never be able to hold onto. Just when we think we might have a grasp on it, it slips from our hands. We compare ourselves to other women constantly, always wanting something we don't have, even if we were content the day before. We spend tons of money on haircuts, clothes, shoes, and take 5,084,484 pictures of ourselves and post them on Facebook.

We are lost in a world of false beauty that is too self-focused to be real beauty. We have to learn to see beauty through God's eyes, not our own.

Also, not matching up to your husband's lustful "ideal" should not determine your own worth. That has nothing to do with your beauty. One man can think something of you, another something else, and God something entirely different than any of them. Why base your beauty on the thoughts of man? There is no man on this earth who could ever know the true depth of your beauty. There is no man on this earth who could ever take God's place. You can't give man the power to validate you in a way only God can. If you do … you will live a miserable life of never measuring up and always wanting to buy the latest Revlon products or pretty clothes. Even if your husband makes you feel like the most beautiful thing in the world … he can never make you feel beautiful like your Creator can.

God does not rate you. The woman who said "God would not be delusional and rate me a 10" was right. He wouldn't do that. Because He doesn't rate us. I asked this because I wanted to see what people believed God thought of them. Obviously, He created us and He thinks we are beautiful, but He does not rate us.

If you want to learn to see yourself through God's eyes, if you want to see yourself as beautiful, you must stop putting words in

Beyond the Mirror

God's mouth. He does not take a few points off when you forget to brush your teeth, or when the kids have you frazzled and your hair is a mess, or when you choose to dress plain and modest, or when you gain a few pounds from pregnancy and have trouble shedding them.

Of course God wants us to take care of our bodies. Our bodies are so important. They aren't just shells, they are temples. They are His and should be taken care of as though they are gifts He literally came down to hand us. If you owned the very sandals Jesus walked in, would you take great care of them? Of course. But those sandals wouldn't lose their value if they got a little mud on them. The value is underneath the mud. Take care of yourself, yes, but don't ever believe that God sees you as less than beautiful because you don't have time to do your hair or go for a run.

Remember, He doesn't think like we do. He doesn't compare us to each other. We are each individually His own creation, intended to serve a purpose only we can serve. No one can take our places. Beauty is about so much more than the physical body. How much do you love people? How much does your heart weep for the poor? How often do you stay up at night fervently praying for your husband's heart to be healed from porn, not for your sake, but for God's and your husband's? How often do you stop thinking about your own insecurities and pray for the hurting hearts of porn stars?

True beauty transcends time. It is not weighed by the culture. It is not weighed by God. It's just not weighed at all. True beauty IS. And although your inner beauty is far more valuable than your outward beauty ... that doesn't nullify the fact that your physical appearance is beautiful. It's your perspective of beauty that is distorted, not your image itself. You're looking at yourself through one of those mirrors at an amusement park. Stop. Look at yourself through God's eyes. When you do that you will see Him in your reflection and not be able to deny the beauty that is there. In this book we are going to dive further into this truth and learn how to look beyond the mirror to find true beauty.

The scale could never, ever be enough to show how beautiful you are. You are beyond 10. You are a creation of God Almighty. The same God who

creates the sunsets we admire and the salty shores we so love. He created you. There is no scale in this world that could capture the beauty of you—only God can.

An Ugly Wife

About a year and a half after George unraveled all of his lies, we went out to eat with friends. Every time we went somewhere in public I scanned the area to make sure no attractive women were in sight.

Well, we walked in to the restaurant and our friends stood right next to a pretty girl. I cringed, wondering if George would think this girl looked prettier than me. As we waited for our table I watched him out of the corner of my eye—every move, every blink. He stood in awkward positions, obviously trying not to look at the girl.

I looked at her every chance I could, soaked in the details of her face, body, eyes, hair. And grew very insecure with each second. Finally, we sat in our seats and this girl happened to sit right behind us. I don't even think George knew that she was seated behind us, but I did. I lost my appetite and barely heard any part of the conversation that night. Then, we went home and I decided to ignore the situation and not bring it up. I thought maybe I could be strong this time, show him that I love him more than myself. Except I didn't love him more than myself. I still cared too much about my own pain. My insecurities were taking over my marriage.

We made love that night. I thought of her, and every other woman I imagined him choosing over me. Meanwhile, George thought we had a great night and that I wasn't going to bring up this girl again. He believed my mask this time.

Over the next few days I grew more insecure. Trust me when I say that I was absolutely hyper-sensitive, insecure, and a little bit on the mentally insane side at this point. I wanted to see that girl's face one more time and know exactly what (if he even did) think was prettier about her.

After torturing myself with thoughts and allowing anger toward George to fester (without even knowing his heart), I talked to him about it.

"Did you double-look at her?" I asked.

It took him awhile, but he admitted.

"Was she pretty?"

Again, it took a lot of prying. He didn't want to say something wrong, but he didn't want to hurt me. I pushed and pushed and pushed. With apprehension in his tone, he finally said, "Yes, she was pretty."

"Was she more beautiful than me?"

"I don't think like that."

"Was she more beautiful than me? You do think like that. I know you do." Again, I accused him without taking time to hear his heart, to know his feelings.

"Actually, she reminded me of you with shorter hair."

Right, I thought. Not what I wanted to hear. I wanted a no. I wanted him to say he didn't know what girl I was talking about. I wanted to be the most beautiful woman in the world to him. My heart bled knowing other women caught his eye. Shouldn't he be so captivated with me that he never, ever notices another woman?

No, the moral of this story is not that I am insane. Although I'm sure that is evident after reading it. The moral here is....

After reading the words above, I know a few things about myself. At that point in life I was extremely ugly, self-centered, insecure, and immature. I loved my husband conditionally. The second he messed up I allowed myself to hate him and accuse him and treat him with no love. I'm not sure why I expected him to love me and treat me as the most beautiful woman in the world when I was far from it. My actions proved one thing:

I cared only about myself at that point.

Yes, he hurt me. Yes, it all started with his unfaithfulness. But I didn't stay true to my vows after he confessed. As he climbed a very steep hill away from lust ... I accused him, shamed him, made him feel like a horrible

husband who would never be able to wipe away his past.

I was emotionally unfaithful. No, I didn't have an affair. Instead, I didn't give him my everything, even after he tried to prove to me countless times that he was on the road to healing.

My point with this is to urge you to realize how often you are being selfish and unloving before we dive deeper into the following chapters. To take responsibility for your own sin and not think you are better than your husband.

Even if someone is unfaithful to us, we should remain faithful. What that faithfulness looks like may depend on the person and situation (obviously we don't sit around while our spouse's beat us to death), but either way, we love. We give. We lay our lives down even when it hurts.

If you are hurting right now because of your husband's battle with lust, I have something to ask of you. I'd like you to lay your life down for your husband (right now, no excuses) without worrying about what he does/doesn't do for you.

Then, I'd like you to write a list of at least 50 things you love about your husband. After that, I'd like you to write down one way you can encourage your husband for each of those 50 qualities. And finally, I'd like you to write a list of at least 50 things you can do for your husband to show him you love him and choose one per day to do for him.

When you are finished the lists give the first list to him, showing him that you've been thinking about his beautiful traits and not just the ugly ones.

Remember … love overcomes all things, but we still have to choose to allow it to work in our lives.

Sensitive to Lust, Not Insecurity

Being sensitive to lustful images, porn, content in movies, and magazine covers is a good thing. Both men and women should be sensitive to these things. But hyper-sensitive?

Hyper-sensitivity will ruin your marriage. I've stopped talking to George simply because he noticed an attractive woman. He didn't lust, didn't linger on any thoughts, nothing. But I accused him of doing what I imagined him to do and refused to believe that he could "notice" an attractive woman without lusting over her.

But when a husband spends so long covering up his lust and lies and porn addiction … it's hard to believe anything he says. So, we make things up. We believe the worst about him and the world. We think there are girls in short skirts on every corner of the street (and sometimes there are!), but in reality we are letting our insecurities get the best of us.

The devil uses a man's lust to break apart a marriage, but he also uses a woman's insecurity. I think women are 5,613 times more physically insecure than men. I really do. We probably compare ourselves to other people way more often than men do. It seems like there are few women in the world who haven't struggled with the I'm not good enough insecurity. We are fed images, mentalities, and standards daily by people who want to change us for some reason.

About a year after I discovered George's secret I would've been labeled hyper-hyper-hyper-hyper-sensitive woman. One day when he was on his way home from work I checked the mail and found a lingerie magazine. I threw it in our trashcan and over the next few minutes I became paranoid

Beyond the Mirror

that he'd find it. So, I dug it out of the bottom of the trashcan and ran out of our apartment door, down the steps in the front lobby, and dropped the magazine at the top of the steps. I figured I'd get it later when he wasn't home and throw it in the dumpster, outside, far from us.

Just my day. He decided to come up those steps that day and saw the magazine I desperately tried to hide. He promised he didn't lust, but I didn't believe him.

Oh, boy.

Hyper-sensitivity will damage you and everyone around you. How can your husband change if you don't give him a chance to? How can he stop lusting after images if you are constantly accusing him of things he's not doing? How can you become more secure in a lustful world if you try to cocoon yourself from everything in the world?

You need to let go of your hyper-sensitive frantic ways. Remember, it's good and wise to be sensitive about what you watch, look at, and let into your heart. It's healthy to be sickened by lust, skimpy clothes, and magazine covers. But … it's unhealthy to take your sensitivity to the extreme and let it tear you apart. Be sensitive to sin because it is evil, but realize that some things in this world hurt and we cannot always avoid them.

You'll have your days, just as I have mine. But there is still hope. You can be better tomorrow than you are today. So can I. We can believe we are beautiful and deeply admire inner beauty more than physical beauty. But first we need to be willing to let go of our craziness and breathe. We need to find freedom to live and let our husband's live, even if that means they are hurting us.

We can't change our husband's heart and we can't change another person's heart—we can only change our own hearts.

That's what's important.

That's what we need to focus on.

So, let's allow God to change our hearts, to rid our hyper-sensitivity and fill it with a deep sadness over sin and lust, and to become a woman of

true beauty. Beauty that doesn't let insecurity damage its existence. Beauty that steps over the devil's schemes with grace, love, and security in Jesus.

Beauty that transcends time.

Self-Insecurity vs. Husband-Insecurity

Way before our husband's walked into our lives there was insecurity in our hearts. For me, it was planted in my heart as a child who never fit in and who could never seem to please people around her. My insecurity was fostered in high school with rejection and comments like, "If you only had _____ then I would like you." I began to look at the world around me and compare myself, constantly, to others. If I had her hairstyle, I'd be loved. If I had her ability to stay organized, I'd be loved.

These insecurities are there, but we sort of give in to them. We try to change or hide behind masks to find love. Or we just hide in general, thinking no one will ever love us for who we are. It's no wonder our world's are shattered when we get married and find out our husband's have cheated on us with images of other women.

He chose me. He held my hand so gently the first day we met. He proposed to me that brisk April night. With watery eyes, he said, "I do," to me that humid July evening. He loved me. I knew he loved me. Then, I found out about the other woman. He didn't really love me. If he did he wouldn't have lied. He wouldn't have wanted her, he would've wanted me.

He chose her.

That is a pain I don't think any man can ever understand. He chose you, only to show you just a little while later that he really chose her—pornography, lust, the other woman. Out of this pain a much deeper insecurity is birthed from the insecurities fostered by our pasts. Self-insecurity, bred by our past wounds, is when we compare ourselves to other women based off of an ideal the world gives us or we create for ourselves based off of our own false perspectives. Self-insecurity is like an endless ache that never seems to be fed. We want to be beautiful and loved.

Well, we assume that our husbands think we are beautiful and loved, although our self-insecurity sometimes throws little doubts in our hearts. But never enough to really hurt us. Until his porn addiction is exposed. Suddenly our self-insecurity is affirmed. We are not good enough. We are not beautiful. Not loved. Not valued for who we are. We are shoved aside for the other woman.

Husband-insecurity is now in the picture. We don't just compare ourselves to other women anymore. We compare ourselves to a specific kind of a woman. The kind of woman we think he prefers. We can't go in public with him without scanning the scene and making sure we see everything he sees. We compare ourselves to everything he sees. Does he think she's prettier than me? Would he rather be married to her? Would he rather have sex with her?

We can't be around our husband's naked anymore. We feel the need to put on makeup before he sees our face. We lock the door when we take showers and dress in the bathroom. We try to control him out of fear. We fear our pain worsening. We fear him continuing to lust. We can't trust him, there's only fear. So we linger there, in fear, as the walls cave in on our hearts and we constantly compare ourselves to others.

Husband-insecurity is so much worse. The one person who should have been faithful, who should have made you feel beautiful and loved … he betrayed you. He chose her. He validated the statement you've heard all of your life, "You're not good enough."

So, you want to please him. You want to be attractive to him. But you don't know how without changing everything about your appearance.

For me, I have shunned the world's view of beauty. I've given up makeup, because it was an idol in my life. I've given up fashion. It was an idol in my life. I've given up everything I've used to try to make the world think I'm beautiful and you know what happened to me? My inner beauty had to stand on its own and I realized just how many flaws I really had. It

went deeper than blemishes and scars on my face. I had so much pride. So much selfishness residing in my heart. My inner beauty, once stripped of its masks, was finally able to be cleansed and renewed.

But now that I've given up the idols in my life and started to seek modesty in my clothing … insecurities will rise because I want to please my husband. I want to catch his eye like the girls who pose temptation.

But why?

There is a self-insecurity and a husband-insecurity. Both live off the same oxygen––a prideful hunger to be the most beautiful woman in the world, to be coveted, admired, looked at, objectified, and for those of us who are too insecure to want to be admired, we want to be accepted. This kind of insecurity is there only when we desire to please the world or our husbands in the wrong way. We shouldn't strive to please our husband's lust or the eyes of this world. We should strive to please God and through that, if we please our husband's, then they know what true beauty is.

That doesn't mean we stop brushing our hair or trying to look feminine and beautiful for our husbands. It does mean, however, that we don't sacrifice modesty for the sake of our insecurities or a desire to please the eyes of lust.

George thinks I'm more beautiful now than he ever did before. He loves that I no longer look to makeup or fashion to determine my worth. He loves that I have a desire to be modest around other men. His heart has truly changed and he loves the change in my heart. But there's still temptation out there trying to get him to lust. And those temptations tempt me to become like them because I know they are eye-catching to my husband. I know there are things in this world he has to look away from, and sometimes I don't like that. My husband-insecurity makes me want to be that something men need to look away from.

But true beauty would never say something like that. True beauty has a humility that snuffs out the passionate flames of self-centered desires for attention or acceptance. True beauty pleases a part of our husbands that reflects God, not the world. True beauty honors God, glorifies Him, and protects other men and women from these same ugly battles. True beauty protects and encourages. It doesn't give in to insecurities caused from the past or a husband's sin. It knows the truth.

That true beauty will live on forever and these masks, this endless striving that is never fulfilled, the desire to be a head-turning object ... it will not last, age or death will eventually rot it, and we will be left with a question about our lives ... did she turn more hearts than heads?

God's Beautiful Garden

In God's garden there are exotic flowers, wild flowers, simple flowers, and not-so-eye-catching flowers. There are so many. And that's what makes a garden so beautiful. A simple, sweet daisy is only meant to fulfill the role of a daisy. If a daisy spends its life trying to be a lily, and a lily spends its life trying to be a rose—who will ever be a daisy? a lily?

It's so important for us to be ourselves. To know and understand who God made us to be and to live that life, not someone else's life. It's also important for us to realize that flowers don't just sit there and look pretty, they are a life source. They serve as the reproduction place for the plant. They are also a source of life and food to insects. We, as women, are not just to be admired for what we look like. We're here to serve a purpose. To be a source of life to those around us. Like a sunflower, we look the Son and reflect His glory to the world around us.

It's beautiful that God desired you in His garden. He knew that it wouldn't be complete without you. But instead of being content in God's garden as the flower He created us to be, we want to jump into an artificial garden filled with plastic flowers that provide no life or reproduction. Why would we want to be part of an artificial garden as opposed to the beautiful, natural garden God has planted us in?

Because the world sells us lies. We forget that being a flower is about more than being a decoration on a dining room table. We get sold on the idea that we are supposed to be pretty little things that are the object of a man's lust or a woman's lust for beauty. So we desire to a part of this artificial garden, thinking we'll feel satisfied, beautiful, wanted, if we kill the real

Beyond the Mirror

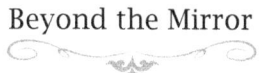

flower and become something fake, something we were never designed to be. But deep down we know that we really don't want this. What we really want is to be exactly where we are, exactly who we are, and someone be completely content in God's garden.

It's just hard when we feel like our husband's desire the artificial garden more than they desire us. We see him glance at an exotic plastic flower and wish we could be as eye-catching. But we forget, so easily, that life is about more than catching eyes.

Insecurity deadens our life as we wilt away. Suddenly the sun is too bright for us and the water isn't quenching. Our desire runs deep. We want to measure up to something we weren't created to be.

What Is Insecurity?

Insecurity is wounded pride. Wounded pride is when our prideful expectations and desires are not met. Our pride is wounded. And our wounded pride gives birth to insecurity. And our insecurity haunts us. Sometimes it feels like it controls us.

I know I have wept countless nights over the insecurity in my life. There's a cold echo in our hearts as we ask ourselves over and over and over, "Why am I not enough?" Why did our husbands, of all people, reinforce this lie we have believed for so long?

You are not good enough. Not pretty enough. Not captivating enough. Not clean enough. Not organized enough. Not tall enough. Not skinny enough. Not curvy enough.

Not.

Enough.

It is heart-wrenching to be a woman sometimes. We are born into a beauty pageant. No need to be Miss America … we're all competing to be Miss The One to our husband's from the day we're born. We can't keep up, so we try harder until we're completely burned out. We don't know how to rest, because we have these expectations to be better. We scan a room when we enter to see if there's a woman who we think is more beautiful that we are. If so, we are miserable the rest of the night. If not, we can rest and be secure with our husbands by our side, knowing that other husband's our admiring us. We cringe when a pretty waitress serves us on a date with our husband. We wonder, we covet, we desire. And all because we have too much pride.

Beyond the Mirror

We want to be the most beautiful flower in the garden. Forget daisies, they're too simple. Forget sunflowers, they're too awkward. Let us be the best, the most admired flower in the garden. But the only problem with that is ... the most admired flower in the garden depends on who you ask. One person prefers the simple daisies. Another is set on the fake, plastic flowers. Another likes roses, even with the thorns. And yet another prefers dandelions.

We have this pride of wanting to be the most beautiful flower. But the most beautiful flower is so relative that it's impossible. It doesn't even exist. So we can compete with each other and try to catch more eyeballs than the next. We can get jealous if our husband's say, "Yes, roses are beautiful in their own way, but I married you, my daisy, and I love everything about you, not just the way you look."

We can say, "That's nice, but I don't want you think any other flowers are beautiful. Just me."

And he will stare at us with a confused look on his face and respond with silence.

We will run off in tears, wondering why, oh why, can't he think every other flower is ugly.

Women are beautiful. Some are exotic. Some are simple. Some are size 0. Some are size 14. But a garden loses its beauty when every flower looks the same.

Our wounded pride will never be content. It will always want something else, something better. It will always want the unattainable goal. To be the most beautiful flower in the garden to every single person in the world, but especially to her husband. This goal becomes so desired that a flower will stop wondering what God thinks of her and just go full-force toward being beautiful to the world.

Insecurity dies when contentment is born. It hates when a flower looks to the Son for nourishment. But what a beautiful day it is when insecurity dies. And then dies every time it tries to spring back up. We have to learn to kill it and to hate it with as much passion as the devil hates us.

How to Kill Insecurity

A flower cannot live without the sun and water. Our desire to be this unattainable beauty is a lust as well. Lust to be beauty. I'm sure a huge part of our lust for beauty comes from the lust men have for the same beauty. It pleases their lust, so we lust after the beauty that pleases their lust.

I think it's so important for us to remember that the beauty we lust over is not a desirable beauty to angels, to Jesus, to our Heavenly Father. It's a beauty this world has fashioned. An unattainable perfection. A scheme to get every woman on earth to search for this unreachable beauty. A scheme to get women to compare, covet, and hate each other. A scheme to get men to desire something they cannot have, so that they never fully desire their wives.

If the devil can keep us all reaching for something that doesn't exist, last, or is completely unattainable, then he knows he will trap us. We will listen to the lies. We will desire things that are not ours. And we will never, ever be satisfied because our goal can never be reached. This goes for men who lust and women who lust over being lusted over.

There is satisfaction, rest, and real beauty in God's arms. There is satisfaction for men who desire purity and love, for women who desire purity and love. For people who desire God. He is the only thing that can fill us, complete us, and allow us to find a state of complete and pure rest. Contentment exists in God. And being the beauty YOU are created to be is the only way you will ever be content in who God made you to be. When you recognize who you are, accept who you are, and decide to stop trying to compete with something that your soul doesn't thirst for.

Beyond the Mirror

Our souls thirst for God. It's only when we try to drink something else that we end up never fully quenched.

Knowing Who You Are

No flower is exactly the same, no matter how much it may look alike. It's not planted in the same exact spot, with the same flowers around it. It's not the same. They are all unique.

You must know who you are in order to be content in who you are. You need to know your strengths and weaknesses. You need to live your own life and remember that life is about more than being pretty. I said this to someone in an email recently and she loved that. It's so true. And there is so much freedom in those words. We are aging, decaying, one day closer to our death … so let's spend these moments living, really living, instead of worrying about the color of our hair or the size of our body parts.

Knowing Who God Is

The biggest and most powerful weapon you have against insecurity is to stop focusing on yourself, who God made you to be, what God thinks of you, what your husband thinks of you, what you think of you, and instead … focusing on God. Who is He? What is He like? How can I be more like Him?

It's important to know who you are in Christ, but you can only know who you are in Christ if you know who Christ is. We need to stop thinking so much about ourselves and think about Him. The more we love Him, the more we won't desire silly earthly things like unattainable beauty. Remember when Paul says that it's better not to marry because when you're married you're too busy trying to please your spouse instead of God? It's so true. We become more concerned with how pretty we are to our man than how much our hearts reflect and glorify Jesus Christ.

But we can look beyond our mirrors. And there, we will find Him, we will find everything we are looking for and so much more.

Your Heart is Damaged

Your heart is hurting right now. Your world feels like it's torn apart. You have a hard time believing anything about your entire marriage, much less something your husband says to you. Your trust for him is below zero. In fact, you barely trust yourself sometimes. You would prefer to spend most of your nights curled up in a ball, crying in bed. But at the same time you don't want him to see your pain. He tries to hold you, you pull away, yet at the same time you really want his embrace.

You just want it to be back to normal, but you don't know what normal is because you've been lied to. You just know you want your marriage to thrive. You want to feel beautiful and loved and you want to love your husband without feeling like you have to guard your heart. You want freedom. Love.

Joy.

But … your heart is damaged.

You are extremely insecure. Your husband's sin has made you set expectations for yourself that are out of this world, not something God would ever ask of you. Because of his addiction to lust, you compare yourself to women and wonder if your husband does the same. You aren't focused on the right things. His struggle with lust has crushed your confidence and left you wondering if you'll ever be enough.

I've been there. I know what it feels like to feel like being single would be so much easier than being married. I know what it's like to desire marriage so deeply, but at the same time feel like men are horrible creatures. I know. I've been there.

Beyond the Mirror

As someone who has seen the darkness a husband's addiction to lust can bring to a marriage, let me tell you this: it doesn't matter what people think of you. It doesn't matter what you think of you when you look at yourself through the eyes of this world. My hope in this book is that you will learn to see yourself through God's eyes and stop caring what people think of you. That you will stop basing your worth and beauty on what your husband sees when he steps out of the house. Even if you have a husband who is unwilling to change in this area (that would be extremely sad and make for a tough marriage) you can still heal in your own heart. I always stress this: your marriage can be suffering because your husband refuses to change, but that doesn't mean your entire being has to suffer, too.

You can believe you are beautiful. And you can stop comparing yourself to other women.

Before your husband came into your life you were probably already forming habits of comparing yourself to other women. His sin has only made this increase in your life. Now you are trying to compare yourself to women that his eyes see AND women you see. It's making you go nuts because you feel like you need to know exactly what every woman he sees looks like, just so you can compare yourself. And what does that do?

It doesn't do anything positive, that's for sure. It makes you feel worse about yourself and it makes him feel like a little boy controlled by his mother. Not healthy for a marriage. Not healthy for your own heart.

I know it's hard because I've been there. I flipped out when George accidentally glanced at a woman, without even lusting. I flipped out when he noticed an attractive girl, then looked away. He didn't dwell, but I blamed him for storing images of women in his head and thinking about them as he looked away. We would walk around in public and he would literally hang his head down and look at the pavement. This always made me feel horrible, too. I used to think, "Wow, are there that many temptations in the world that you have to look at your feet all the time?"

He couldn't win. Why? Because I loathed the fact that he had temptations. I wanted him to never be tempted. I wanted to be so much of enough to him

that no woman in the world could tempt his eyes to look.

This is so impossible. It's just crazy to expect that of a man. And we can't expect that, even though it would make us feel so much better.
But it's not the case. We ALL have temptations. Just like women are tempted to be jealous and compare, men are tempted to lust. It doesn't mean they lust when they are tempted. They can overcome these temptations, but the devil is always going to be trying to get us to fall. That's why we have to be careful about what we let into our hearts and minds.

Your husband should be willing to give you a detailed account on a pad of paper of every woman he sees every day … he should be willing to do anything to make you feel better. But I urge you to reconsider asking him to do crazy things. Why would you do that to yourself? Why do you want to make him even more aware of women around him? I did this very thing to George. Told him to come home and tell me everything he saw, in detail. Not everything he lusted over, just everything he saw. I wanted to know hair color, eye color, if she was prettier than me. And he told me. Every day.

Know what happened to me? I became the most insecure, unhappy, world-focused woman in the world. It made me so focused on what I looked like that I couldn't even focus on real life. I was too consumed by wanting to buy better clothes, or dye my hair, or whatever. I compared myself to these women he would describe to me and I felt like dirt. Every time we made love I thought of those women. Every day he came home from work we spent our night discussing other attractive women. Is that really how you want to spend your marriage? It broke us to pieces. I'm surprised God could even heal us after all that, but He has.

Please, consider how you are allowing your insecurities to damage yourself further (and now affect your marriage). These insecurities would be there regardless of being single or married. When you are married they are heightened, even without porn. But once this porn stuff enters and the lies and all that are exposed … it is much worse. It makes you lose your mind. It makes you go crazy. It makes you want to attach a camera to your husband's shirt so you can see everything he sees all day and drive yourself crazy insecure comparing yourself to every woman, wondering if he thinks she is prettier than you.

Beyond the Mirror

Here is a fact: To the world, there are many women in the world that look better than you. There are many women in the world that look better than me. In the world's eyes. God doesn't compare us like we compare ourselves. To Him, none of us look better, because we all look like a perfect version of ourselves. We are to live out ourselves, not try to be like everyone else.

Why spend your life caring about the external and comparing yourself? There are so many beautiful women in this world — why bother wasting time comparing ourselves to women when we could be spending time on things that truly matter? Like growing closer to God, increasing the beauty of our inward character, mothering beautiful babies, serving our husbands?

Seek God. INTENSELY. Journal to Him throughout your day. Immerse yourself in things that matter. Read stories of Christian people throughout the centuries who have DIED for Jesus. Realize that there is so much more to this life than the surface. And life with God isn't just about loving Him and praying at night … it's also about DYING so that you may truly live. You need to let the parts of yourself die that you're still holding onto. You need to die to this world and you need to lay your life down for God, then your husband.

Be serious about this or you are going to keep going in circles until you end up signing divorce papers. That means the devil wins. Don't let him win. Fight. Live. Love. Find hope beyond all this mess by looking to God and letting those parts you are trying to control GO. Live for others, for God … focus less on yourself.

I really believe you can find hope. It's all a matter of being willing to let go of the things that are ruining your marriage. Lust and insecurity together are deadly. As you are experiencing now. Don't let it kill your love. Remember why you said those vows in the first place. Love CAN overcome this, and it WILL … if you choose it.

Your Beauty Defined

As you look in the mirror and cover up your flaws, what are you thinking? Do you do this casually without thought, or do you consciously try to cover your flaws?

Both men and women have a tendency to hide flaws. That's often why men hide porn and women hide their jealousy behind false confidence. We clean up our houses before guests or apologize for the mess when someone comes by unannounced. And when we're caught without one of our masks there is actually an anxious feeling produced. Oh no, someone is going to see my messy house, my unpainted face, my frizzy hair, my messy car, the crumbs all over the kitchen floor. We love our masks. They help us feel safe from the world's glaring eyes. They help us feel confident, even if it's fake.

We let the world define our beauty. The beauty of our houses, our faces, our bodies, and all that we are. Our ideals of perfection are unattainable and completely unrealistic, which is why we never feel like we measure up and we just keep striving.

Ah, there is rest. There is so much rest in saying, "World, people, self, I am no longer giving you the authority to define my beauty or worth." Lay aside the idea of perfection in the world's eyes and peel off the masks. Welcome someone into your messy home with a smile and say, "I spend more time making memories with my kids than I do cleaning." Venture out of the house without makeup on your face and say, "World, I am beautiful without hiding your idea of flaws."

And here's the real kicker. Learn to see flaws as beautiful. Stop buying into the messages commercials and advertisements shoot at your heart.

Battle those lies with truths. You need concealer for the circles under your eyes VS. I am beautiful just the way God created me.

Aging is beautiful to God, not to the world. Flaws are beautiful to God, because they show that His perfection is the only true perfection. If we keep hiding our flaws we are really just trying to be fake gods who want their perfection worshiped. But we aren't perfect. That is the truth. And in that truth there is rest. Worship God, true perfection, and learn to see flaws as a way to bring glory to God. Don't hide from your imperfections. Hiding only hurts your heart, brings anxiety, and leads other people into the same dark tunnel of endless striving. The more we hide, the more we urge others to hide.

Be honest. Open. And transparent. Show the world that it's okay to be who God made you to be. We don't have to strive. We don't need to hide. What we all really need is to smash the world's ideal and make our ideal line up with God's, not the world's. Anytime you feel insecure or hear a lie in your heart, battle it with the truths of God's word. We'll go into more detail of this in the latter half of the book.

One of my biggest hopes is that you can find the freedom to LIVE again. To get rid of the anxiety that comes with endless striving and rest in who you were created to be.

Modesty of Heart

Modesty to me isn't about your clothes. It's about your heart. There are plenty of women who think they are modest. They cover up from neck to ankle, but they don't carry themselves with humility. They still have so much makeup on their faces that you wonder what they really look like, they still flaunt their looks, and they still, whether they want to think so or not, are treating their own beauty as an idol. We can't know for sure when we look at someone and it's not up to us to judge, but if we really allowed God to show us the true colors of our own hearts we would realize that we are a lot less modest than we think we are.

I have met very, very few women who model true modesty. Some model the outward characteristics, but lack the heart. The women I have met who truly live from a heart of modesty don't care what others think of them. I have yet to reach this myself, although I am so hungry for it.

They are the type of women who would never post a million pictures of themselves online for the world to stand in awe of. They could be completely beautiful, but you'd never think that when talking to them. You'd be so in awe of the light of Christ reflecting from them that their faces wouldn't even matter. I don't know of many women who are like this.

So many women are consumed with fashion, makeup, dying their hair, having 5,274 pictures of themselves, getting rid of grays, finding the best skin products, etc. They are more interested in losing weight than losing sin. This is why I truly believe that modesty is something that starts with the heart. A humble heart will naturally appear modest in every way, from speech to clothing. What that looks like for each person, I don't know.

But I do know that this kind of modesty is rare. We live in a culture where even Christian women are told to look stylish, but modest. Be totally into fashion, like, you know, but just cover up the cleavage and thighs. That's all modesty is. Coverage. I'm sorry, but I disagree. We've tried to find this balance of looking good and looking modest. But if we're still trying to look good … haven't we lost the true beauty of a modest and humble woman?

I know of a few women who have modesty of heart and they are the most beautiful women I know. My hope is to be one of them. Right now, I'm not. I still care too much, but my hope is to be humbled to the point that the only thing a mirror reflects is Jesus Christ's beauty in me. More of Him, less of me. Modesty is such an annoying term to me nowadays. It's about so much more than covering up certain parts of the body. I'm done with this culture's view of modesty. I want something deeper. So, I've given up the term modesty in my heart's vocabulary. Instead, I am after humility.

Unnoticed to the World, Noticed to God

Immodesty is a need/desire to seek your value/worth in anything other

Beyond the Mirror

than God. The need to adorn yourself to feel beautiful. The need to hear people tell you that you're beautiful in order to feel beautiful. And really, the need/focus on outward beauty in general. We should desire to find our value and contentment in God. No, that doesn't mean we ponder what God thinks of us and view ourselves through that perspective. It means we stop thinking about what we look like, what we don't look like, what we should look like, and we focus on God. We stop looking inward and we look up. We should be so focused on Him that the last thing we care to think about is our reflections in the mirror or our appearances to the world

To be modest you don't need to look in the mirror and figure out if your jeans show us the shape of your body, you simply need to stop looking in the mirror and look up. Stop scanning the closet for something that will make men turn their heads and make other women admire you. And if you are like me, if you have a problem with placing your worth in your appearance, throw out your wardrobe and wear the same thing every day.

Clothing, makeup, outward appearances—they too often become idols to us. We so desperately want to please the world that we don't desire humility. Instead, we cultivate a desire for pride and recognition. Our goal should be to love God so intensely that we desire humility. That's a tough thing to desire.

Humility ... insignificant, unnoticed, unappreciated, lowly, meek. It's not often you meet someone who says, "Yes, I'd like to be unnoticed and insignificant." Instead, we want to be noticed, admired, loved, valued, appreciated, etc. We want the world to think we're special more than we want God to think we're special. We cry over this. We freak out about what our husband's look at because of this. And yet we don't have nearly the same passion to be a better example of Christ.

Modesty, true modesty, isn't about having all of your skin covered up. It's about desiring Jesus Christ more than anything in the world. It's obsessing over Him more than we do our appearances to our husband's and others. It's forgetting the world, forgetting how many shoes we have, and giving all we have to our God. Modesty is a need and desire to seek your value fully in God.

So, instead of thinking what to wear, what not to wear, how long the dress should be, think about God and wrap yourself completely in Him. I've met plenty of women who are covered from neck to ankle, but have no true modesty, humility, gentleness, or beauty about them. They simply have dress codes. Don't make modesty about dress codes. A truly modest woman is humble in appearance because of the humility in her heart. Her modesty springs from her humility. And when you look at her there you don't see a reflection of the latest fashions, you see the reflection of Jesus Christ.

That's what I want to be. Unnoticed to the world, but noticed to God. A reflection of all that He is.

Behind the Lies

Appearance to the World

We strive, so endlessly, to be beautiful. We hide, so purposefully, our flaws, our dreams, and our realities. Because we want to be enough.

The heart of a woman affected by porn has also been affected by the world. This is why her husband's sin really, really wounds her. And this is why it's so important for the man in her life to step up and fight for her, not against her. He can either be a tool to wound her further, or a tool to aid in the healing her wounds and help her rest in who God made her to be.

But this doesn't change the fact that the way we have been affected by the world has caused great pride in us. A former pastor of ours once referred to insecurity as wounded pride. Think about that. You have a prideful desire to be beautiful and alluring, and when the desire feels unmet you put on more make-up, buy more clothes, whatever you can to fulfill this desire. And when it still isn't satisfied you are left with wounded pride—insecurity.

We can use our insecurity wounds as excuses for our husband's to stop sinning and treat us right, but that's not a beautiful or admirable quality. We are expecting our husband's to nurse our pride. I often wonder why we aren't more concerned with our husband's thinking our virtue is beautiful.

Think about it. Throughout this process of lust and betrayal, we like to believe that our husband's sin is the reason we are so insecure, so unbeautiful feeling. But really … it's not just his actions. It's our actions throughout our entire lives as well. We worship ourselves. I know it feels better to be the pitied one throughout all of this pain. The one who is good, while the husband is the horrible sinner. But we both are. Both husband and wife worship themselves. That's why the man is so wrapped up in self-pleasure and objectifying women. That's why the woman is so wrapped up in being physically beautiful to an unattainable perfection. And when this pride of ours is wounded … our insecurity spreads like a wild fire.

This world. I really think it causes so many lies in our hearts to be seen as truths. And I think men buy into the world's view of beauty. It allures them. They treat women, even their wives, as objects. And in turn, we want to be objects to a degree. We like when head's turn, when other women want something we have, and we so value our husband's praise about our physical appearances. There's nothing wrong with physical beauty. Women are physically beautiful. And you know … so are flowers, and men, and children. But we so often refuse to rest in who we are, in the beauty God gives us, and instead we strive after something the world created, something unreachable.

So we hide our real, natural beauty, and we strive for a beauty we will never attain. We value sexiness more than virtue. And we wound ourselves when we allow wounded pride to take over our hearts.

The False Self

Underneath all of these layers there is a "true self." Most of us don't even know who we really are. So often we don't even realize we are living as a false self. That's how thick the masks are. This false self is fashioned by our consent to our surroundings. Sometimes we are too young or naïve to realize we are consenting to these things. And by the time we become adults there are so many layers over our true selves that we can't begin to fathom who we really are. So we give in and believe we are who we want to be. If someone makes fun of us, we believe it and feel bad about ourselves, or we change it to feel better about ourselves. In turn, we miss out on who we really are. We're too busy living up to our parent's, boyfriend's, husband's, best friend's, even our own expectations, that we lose who we really are.

This world requires much of you. Constant change, an ageless figure, an immaculate house, the right parenting decisions, you have to spank or not spank depending on who you are surrounded by. Every decision you

make is scrutinized by the world and spit out in disgust. The world hates your decisions, no matter what they are, purely so that you continue striving and never grow content in who you are. The more masks you have, the more you care about your appearance to the world, well, the more products you buy.

Your false self throws a party and strives after unattainable things. It's no wonder so many of us suffer with depression. We are living lies and never measuring up anyway. No matter what we do … we fail. That is depressing!

The Real Self

It's not just about being counter-cultural. And it's not just about resting in who God created you to be. It's about re-channeling your striving toward worldly "perfection." Instead of worrying about your appearance to the world, you concern yourself with the appearance of your soul to God. What does He see in the darkest corners of your heart?

Instead of striving toward the world, press on toward God. The closer you draw near to His presence, the hotter the flames will get. Your lies can't stand these flames, so you my want to run as far as you possibly can in the other direction. But it's only through the flames of God's holiness that your masks can be peeled off, one by one.

For me, I drew near to God and recognized my issues with vanity and pride. I used makeup and fashion to feel better about myself. And I had to recognize that George's issues with porn and lust were not the "source" of my insecurities. They were another arrow in the same wound, but not the source.

Stripping Pride

My insecurity was birthed from pride. They are nothing more than my prideful expectations or desires not being met. I wanted to be the most beautiful woman in the world to my husband. Literally. I didn't want him to even think another woman was attractive in any way. I didn't want to

Beyond the Mirror

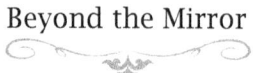

be the standard for his view of beauty, I wanted to be the only beauty to him. It's impossible, but I wanted it. I didn't even care about inner beauty at that point. I was purely focused on being outwardly alluring in the ways "the other women" were. Even his appreciation for the beauty of nature bothered me when I was at this point. I truly wanted to be the only physical thing he thought was beautiful.

So ... I got rid of makeup. I knew it was a mask in my life. I knew it was an idol. Something I needed to feel good about myself. I didn't intend to get rid of it forever, just long enough to no longer need it. But when I stopped wearing it my heart started to change. I realized how beautiful inner beauty is and how fake the beauty of this world is. I wanted more inner beauty. I haven't worn makeup since. In the past I'd try not to be too public about this because I don't want other women to feel they need to do the same thing. I know it's extreme. But it's what I, personally, needed to do in my own life to get over this. For me, I am a very extreme person, and that makes me extreme about getting rid of the lies and sin in my own heart. I don't want anything to do with it. And the more women I talk to who are hurting because of other women who flaunt their beauty instead of being humble ... I really, really have trouble desiring to be a part of that cycle.

But, even with makeup out the window, I still had issues. So, being the extreme person that I am, I said, "Lord, I don't want to be focused on outward beauty at all. I want to be beautiful inside and never be noticed or admired for what I look like." I got rid of my entire wardrobe so that fashion could no longer be something I used to "feel good about myself." I had one simple style of a dress that I wore every single day. (Now, I don't recommend this to anyone. This is just an inside glimpse into the extreme measures I took to get over my own issues. Please, search your own heart and don't ever feel like you need to follow in my footsteps.)

Do you know how much this has changed me? When I go out I don't think about other men or women looking at me, because I don't spend time trying to look like something worth staring at. I don't stare at other women anymore, wishing I could be like them, because I'm not focused on my outward beauty anymore. I know God made me beautiful. He makes all women beautiful. But I no longer focus on it. We have one mirror in our house and it has an image of Jesus on it so that I can only see my reflection by looking through Jesus.

Freedom in Christ

I don't want to be a woman who spends her life searching for a physical beauty that's never going to last. I want to enjoy aging and love every gray hair that comes my way. I don't want to focus on diets and losing weight and fearing what another pregnancy might do to me. Instead, I want to devote my life to others and never be concerned about what I look like. Now, I don't walk around looking like a homeless person. My hair is brushed, my skirt is beautiful and feminine, and my shirts are not George's old t-shirts. I dress like a woman.

So, this has changed me immensely as far as insecurities go. I don't watch TV or movies that would cause me to dwell on these things. I don't stare at magazine covers in the grocery store line. In fact, I don't even glance at them. I can't tell you the latest celebrities. I don't allow tons of images to be put into my head that will make me jealous and prideful. So when these things do come into my path, they nudge at my wounds, but it's rare that the wound is re-opened. My battle with insecurities is just as much of a battle as George's battle with lust. We will always have temptations to be jealous or lust (both are coveting another woman in some way), but we can choose not to give into those things and we can choose to do things that will prevent those temptations from happening as often.

That's what I've done. As extreme as it is to some ... it works for me. I've finally come to a place where I am content to be me, but still striving to become more like Christ, and less like me. And I love the freedom in it. The freedom in knowing that I don't need to worry about what others think of me, I just need to please God. And through pleasing God, through repentance and obedience, I am becoming more and more like Him.

Now, who knows what path you need to take to get to this point. God will lead you. Be willing to let go of your pride in ways you just don't want to. Humility does not come without a little humiliation. Seek humility and rid your masks. You'll find great freedom in being less concerned with your outward beauty and more concerned with being beauty in everything you do.

Wouldn't it be so beautiful if all of us were so reflective of God's beauty that every person who met us couldn't recall what we looked like on the outside? That's my greatest desire. To reflect more of Him to the world, and less of me. It's through reflecting His beauty that we reach the truest state of ourselves, living out the very thing we were created to be ... images of God.

False Humility & Self-Pity

So often we associate humility with ignoring a compliment, covering up our beauty, or being transparent and giving people way too many details about our lives. Humility isn't attained by our personal efforts. It's impossible. The more we try to attain it, the more we will be focused on it, and there, with the realization of our humility, we will find our pride. "Look how awesome I am, I'm humble."

It doesn't make sense.

Another thing we often associate humility with is self-pity. *Oh, I'm just horrible. Oh, I'm just a terrible mother. Oh, my husband cheated on me and poor, poor me.* We don't accept our pain and treat it as a means to make us more like Christ. Instead, we clutch onto our pain and hope the world admires us for it.

We focus on our own flaws and the flaws of others and we dwell there as the humble servant who can't get anything right. But self-pity is another form of pride. You can know this by the fruit of self-pity. It doesn't bring peace to self or others. It isn't focused on God. And it generally leaves you with a prideful feeling of, "Hey, I wonder if anyone is noticing my pain." And if people don't notice how wronged you have been and how "well" you are handling it, you will get upset. It's inevitable. You want to be praised because you are the victim. Praise is what you are after. To be thought well of by those around you. Or simply to be pitied.

The Best Medicine for Self-Pity

Every day I drenched my sheets in tears. Every day that I rounded up the energy to shower, I tasted my tears mingled with the running water. My tears. They became my best friend, my most consoling source. I hated crying back then, but it flowed from me all the time. When George went to work, tears. When he went to the gas station with all the magazines staring at him, tears. When he saw a pretty waitress, tears.

Sometimes those tears turned to anger, but most times they led me down a path of self-pity that could have easily ruined me. I worried constantly–c-o-n-s-t-a-n-t-l-y–about what my husband saw. I analyzed women everywhere I went, even when George wasn't with me. I compared myself. I wallowed there in my self-pity because I fed my insecurity every chance I could, instead of feeding my desire for God. I was more focused on myself–what I lacked and what I wanted–instead of focusing on God.

I wanted. But I didn't receive. So I wallowed.

Feeding this self-pity will turn it into a beast. You'll end up on anti-depressants. You'll end up spending tons of money on psychology sessions. You'll end up so dependent on anything to keep you going, instead of depending solely on God, the only One who can fill, satisfy, and heal us.

Healing doesn't happen when we turn to anti-depressants to relieve our self-pity. (Sure, there may be times medication is necessary, but I'm only speaking of self-pity right now.) There is no man-made medicine for self-pity. There's no will power that can climb out of the quicksand of self-pity. Your medicine for self-pity is to love God more. To love others more than you love yourself. To be more focused on what you can do for God and others than what they can do for you. To give up your rights and desires and surrender to God's will for your life. To give up and give God the reigns.

I knew I was about to experience a big change in my life and marriage when my pillows were saturated because I was mourning my own sin, instead of wallowing in self-pity. When I recognized my own sin, my own need for God, and my own lack of dependency on Him … I could have done two things. 1.) I could have turned from God and tried harder to fix things on my own. 2.) Or, I could have turned to God and loved Him more, allowing love for Him and His love for me to transform me.

Ashley Weis

I chose the second and it has made all the difference. I stopped taking my own medicine for self-pity and turned to God. I rested in His love and gave Him my heart. Being in love with my King is the only thing that has saved me (and continues to save me) from a marriage destroyed by pride. And I recommend the same medicine for you.

Busy Little Bees

We all have busy lives as it is. Whether it's kids or a career, laundry or bills, we're busy. And we don't stay busy, we get busier. Especially when the dots around us don't line up as straight as like we'd like them to. When our world falls apart (when we fall apart) we hide in chores, hobbies, even acts of kindness and volunteer work. We fear the unspoken message of silence, so we keep the lights on and run on empty until we crash (or don't crash because our minds are too busy to sleep).

When people ask us how we're doing we reply with the generic, "Good. How are you?" Never in a million years would we say, "Actually I'm really struggling with insecurities right now because my husband cheated on me." No, of course not. We couldn't say that. Then people would know we're not perfect.

But people don't have time to get to know our tears if we hide behind work, work, work. Faith is dead without works (James 2:17), and in our hiding, lack of faith thrives in the motivations that drive our actions. The motivation being our own inability to display our weaknesses to ourselves and others. To be real.

I am convinced that our lack of humility is one of the main reasons so many pastors and people sitting in the pews every Sunday are involved with pornography. It's not the only reason. But it's one of them. We go to church, help out in the nursery, preach a sermon, work with the youth, go to our small groups, but behind the scenes we're weak, hurting, and bloated with pride. Our souls are thirsting for righteousness, but our minds are too busy being busy. Too dedicated to hiding behind the mask of good works to realize just how weak and in need of God we really are.

The Great and Wondrous Distractions

Take an average person from our current culture and put them in the desert, alone, for an entire month. No cell phones, no radios, no gadgets and gizmos galore. Just the soul surrounded by nature and God. It could be a good thing for this soul, but given the current culture and our need for distractions buzzing in our ears, I'd say this person would have an incredible chance of leaving the desert in need of major psychiatric help.

We're distracted and we like it that way. People check their email and social media accounts first thing in the morning. A huge percentage of people have conversations via text and Twitter or Facebook more than they do in person or the phone. Last summer I rocked my youngest baby on the porch almost 24/7. During those times I'd see moms walk by with their cell phones glued to their fingers (no longer the ears) as their children lagged behind, kicking rocks and wondering why there's never any time to smell the roses.

I told myself, "Self, you will never do that." And yet, I've done it so many times since then. Ignored my children to send a text message. It's all part of our masks. Our false selves trying to keep their heads above the surface while our real selves drown in the sea of noise.

These distractions may not seem like a big deal throughout our day. We listen to the radio on the way to work. We answer text messages while we play with our kids. We live our lives and think of how great of a blog post our interesting moments will make. We think of a clever sentence and grab our cell phones to let Twitter in on the action. It seems harmless. But so does a little clutter on the dining room table, until the clutter turns into a mountain, and the mountain spreads to the kitchen, then the stairs, the bed room, the laundry. The mountain grows until our house is in need of a major spring cleaning.

Our souls are in need of a major spring cleaning. If we allow these distractions to build into mountains we will never be able to stand before

Ashley Weis

God with purity of heart. Jesus said those who are pure in heart will see God. To see God, we need less distractions, less masks, and more of Him. A major spring cleaning that rids us of all of our masks.

Helping out at church, running all over the state to check out the latest yard sales, giving 80% of your money to charities, adopting 147 million orphans ... those are wonderful things even when done for the wrong reasons. However, filling our lives with "good works" while lacking faith is not going to get us anywhere. We will stand in the same place our entire lives. Running so fast on a treadmill as the world passes us by. And when it's all said and done we'll be known as a good person, but will we be known as a person who lit the world with the light of Christ?

Will we be known as people who knew when to say no to outside obligations so that we could get our hearts right with God? Will we be known as people who helped the homeless, but neglected our wounded relationships with our husbands, family, and friends? Will we be known as people who hide our weaknesses behind good works, or people who have so much faith and love for God that our actions overflow with the fruits of the Spirit?

Don't let your pain keep you from loving God without distraction. Don't allow your fear of insecurities and weaknesses to rob you from relying fully on God. Accept your shortcomings and stand before God honestly, asking Him to transform those very weaknesses.

Being beautiful isn't equal to being busy. Someone once said to me, "I just feel like I need to get my mind set on others. I need to help out at church more or something." I wrote back to this email and said, "Don't you already help out at church quite a bit?" She responded, "Yes, of course, but I just need to do more. I need to get outside of myself and focus on others, so that I stop dwelling in my own pain."

On the surface this seems like a good idea. Be others-centered, not self-centered. If we help others we won't have time to be insecure. If we dissect this, however, we can see that the reason for being others-centered is self-centered. It's done out of an effort to get rid of our own pain. It's not done purely out of love for the other person. So what seems others-centered is actually self-centered. And because of this, you are only ignoring pain, not dealing with it.

Judgment & Comparison

How often have you been uncomfortable around another woman because she looked up and down, assessing what you looked like? How often have you been the woman who walks into a room with her husband and assesses everyone around you in order to make sure you are the most beautiful woman there? How often has your security in public (or during a movie) depended on what the other women look like?

We are caught in a daze. We judge people based on their appearances without giving much thought to their souls. Perfect example. Porn stars. We're too busy judging them for what they do and how they look to realize that they are hurting and in need of love and compassion. I'm so glad that God doesn't see people like we do. We look at the outward appearance, but He looks at the heart (1 Samuel 16:7).

Sometimes we judge others to feel better about ourselves. If we put others down, we elevate ourselves. We don't even need to slander in front of others, we can do it in our own minds and still feel better about ourselves. It's interesting that we put others down to feel better about ourselves, but at the same time we compare ourselves to women we think are better than us and end up slandering ourselves, too. We are caught up in judging, comparing, and coveting. An empty, worthless cycle that will lead us to despair and crush our hearts to pieces.

Those of us with swollen pride strive to be sexy, to be wanted for our looks. And we'll do whatever it takes, wear whatever it takes, to feel wanted. Those of us with injured pride strive to be hidden. Being noticed for our looks makes us feel uncomfortable, most of the time at least. We don't want

Beyond the Mirror

to be an object, but at the same time we want to be noticed and loved while being hidden. We want someone to find us, rescue us, and make us feel safe. Both swollen pride and injured pride lead us to the same place. An endless and impossible search for the world's validation.

Freedom from this cycle only comes when we surrender our quest for self-worth and decide that we would rather preoccupy ourselves with God's worth than even consider our own worth. In Him, we know our worth. We know that we are created in the image and likeness of God Himself. To think less of ourselves is to think less of God.

It's not so much about raising our self-esteem as it is wiping our self-esteem away and focusing on God's beauty. Stepping away from the mirror and kneeling in front of our Maker, asking Him if, through His grace, He could make us consumed with His beauty instead of our own.

Beyond the Mirror

We stare in mirrors a lot. In my past I often spent 2 hours in front of a mirror to prep myself for the world. Yes, that's 2 hours of staring off into space, sprinkled with many thoughts of self-admiration. Wow. I started spending between 30 minutes and 2 hours in front of the mirror at the age of 13. I stopped when I was 23 years old. If we average 30 minutes and 2 hours we get 75 minutes. Multiply that by 365 days in a year and we get 27,375 minutes, that's 456.25 hours in a year. Now, let's multiply that by 10.

In my life I have spent approximately 4,562 hours admiring or feeling bad about myself (that's 273,750 minutes). Now, thankfully I only did this for 10 years. And I'm now blessed because we only have one mirror in our house (which has Jesus painted on it, so you can only see your reflection when looking through His) and I look in the mirror so often that I forget what I look like. Not saying you have to do the same, but I don't want to add any more hours of self-admiration to my already enormous number. And I know myself well enough to know that I could not look in a mirror for 5 minutes without admiring myself. Imagine if I continued in this pattern

until I was 50. Then I'd have spent 18,240 hours of self-admiration or self-deprecation that made me feel empty.

No, thank you. There is life beyond the mirror. That's the life I'm thirsty for. Jesus Christ. Oh, how sorry I am that I wasted 4,562 hours of the life He gave me. That's not even including the times I've taken pictures of myself with my phone, looked in the mirrors in my car and public bathrooms, stared at pictures of myself, spent time rehearsing for my Grammy speech in front of the mirror, went tanning, paid over $30 for a hair cut, paid over $80 to have my hair colored, shopped for clothes that made me feel better about myself, and I can't forget the many times I looked at buildings that revealed my much sought after reflection as I walked by.

If I calculate the estimated amount of hours I've set aside for prayer … well, let's see, I've spent 608 hours of my life between the ages of 13 and 23 in set-aside time for prayer. That's 3,954 more hours in front of a mirror than in front of Christ during those 10 years.

Enough said.

Appearance to Self

The heart of a woman goes back to the little girl splashing in puddles. Not every little girl is like her. Some have been abused and beaten down by the world before they wake up to their fifth birthday. Those little girls don't live. They hide. Like we do now.

We don't want to hide, though. We don't want to tire ourselves as we strive to be someone we're not. Someone we think is better. We want to rest. Freedom. Freedom to be ourselves. Freedom to be enough without putting on a mask or being rejected. That's what we want. But the world steals our freedom and laughs in our faces.

Before I met George, guys I dated told me qualities I needed in order to be good enough for them. One guy told me he couldn't pursue a relationship with me because I lacked qualities he wanted.

"What qualities?" I asked, over the phone, wondering at the same time why I'd ask such a question.

"Well, a flatter stomach and whiter teeth. And I'd like your hair to be your natural color, without the highlights."

"Okay." I sighed, trying to hide the pain of being rejected.

I toned my stomach, whitened my teeth, and dyed my hair before I saw that guy again. But I didn't let him back into my heart. I wanted to show him that the things he wanted were things that change, things that shouldn't determine the worth of someone. If only I would've truly believed that myself, but boy after guy after man in my life affirmed the opposite. I needed to change to be good enough.

Once, a guy told me I needed to worship with my hands raised and furrow my brow. He also wished I were sportier and better at volleyball. Sorry, but I'm not. And even though this guy wasn't my ideal man, the rejection still sunk an arrow into my wound. My not good enough wound. It's not just physical beauty or inner beauty we want. We want to be ourselves and be loved for who we are. You can imagine why I was so devastated when porn knocked on the door of my marriage. Again, I wasn't enough.

A friend of mine was recently set up on a blind date. She got upset when the guy didn't pursue her.

"What do you think of our relationship?" She asked him, hoping for him to sweep her off her feet.

"How can I think much of anything at this point?" He said. "We've only been on two dates." Not exactly the answer she wanted to hear. She got upset and told him to call her when he knew what he wanted. He didn't call her for days. Their short-lived dating relationship ended before it had a chance to begin, and one of the last things he said to her was, "I don't think this is worth pursuing."

That kind of rejection hurts. It's not about the guy thinking we are beautiful or not. None of us will be perfect in the world's eyes. We are given standards for beauty and weight and homemaking and raising children that no one in this world could live up to. We can exhaust ourselves trying, but we'll miss out on life. What we really want is to be content in who we are. But it's so difficult when people in our lives constantly tell us we aren't enough. It's hard to shake off the rejection of someone telling you in some way that you are not worth fighting for.

This is why our hearts drop when we see our husband's drool over another woman. Not because we want to be the most achingly beautiful woman in the world. It's more than that. We want to be enough as we are. We want someone to say, "It's okay. There's no need to strive. You are lovely as you are." But we're told that we won't be enough unless we buy more makeup, pay $19.99 a month to get bronze skin, wear the right clothes, talk quieter or louder depending on who you ask, submit to our husbands, become doormats, home school our kids and do so perfectly, … again, the lists goes on forever.

Based off the lies and messages the world feeds us, we create standards to live by. Standards that will make us feel like enough. Until someone else gives us something to change.

Wanting to Be Someone Else

You are you. I am me. Profound, isn't it? Not really. As simple as this is, we make it so complicated. We our fed these lies, so we create standards to live up to in order to feel like we look better to ourselves and to the world. Validation is what we're talking about here.

But this kind of validation isn't found in who God created you to be and who He wants to transform you to be by becoming more like Him. This validation isn't a validation of who you really are. It's a validation in the you that you want to be. It's found in the approval of self and others. And generally, your own approval of yourself is based on how you think other people view you.

This is where the change comes in. The desire to be someone else. Someone "better." This could be anything from piling makeup on to getting breast implants to cleaning up our houses before guests arrive to flaunting our amazing taste in unique music. Anything that is not who we are, but is who we want to be. This "who we want to be" is what we talked about earlier, our false self.

This self pleases the world. It makes people feel comfortable, because this self conforms to the people it is around. If a brunette marries a man who likes blondes, her false self will either dye her hair blonde or compare herself to every blonde she sees in order to conform to the likes of her husband. And in turn, she may feel validated for a little while, but underneath the hair dye she is hiding her true self. How depressing.

The more we try to please the world and lust (which both change all the time), the more we'll go in circles and never find rest for our souls. We will chase after something that cannot be attained. And we'll only feel good about ourselves when we're wearing whichever mask the person around us wants us to wear.

There is no freedom in this.

Shattering the Delusion

Appearance to God

There's one question I often ask couples. They flood me with questions. Is the beach okay? Are video games? Movies? Rated-R movies? What about X-Rated if look away during bad parts? Can we go to Target? Should we hang out with people who constantly talk about other women and men like it's no big deal? There are endless questions when it comes to this stuff. But my one question to you is ... what kind of heart do you have?

Right now we'll talk about two different hearts. One is a heart that makes other people feel comfortable and at home. People who curse God don't even feel the slightest bit unwelcome. It's a soothing heart to those who don't love God. This heart can tell you about the latest TV shows and video games, the weather, the latest celebrities, and will laugh at all your dirty jokes. It's a heart that is tainted by the world. A heart that welcomes the world and shuns Jesus Christ.

It's not that Jesus doesn't want to dwell in this heart, but He has no room there. He's tried to creep in, but He gets pushed aside for the latest news. Even if He did creep in, He couldn't stay long. This kind of heart is too dirty for Him. It isn't clean or pure. It's entertained by movies that use His name in vain. Entertained by lust, lies, and murder–things He doesn't love. Things He died to clean. This heart feels moments of pleasure and fulfillment. Sometimes even gets the best "lot" in life. The best cars, looks, jobs. Tons of money and popularity. But this heart is lacking something that is crucial. And yet, you can tell this heart all you want, but it would rather stay the way it is than have Jesus dwell inside.

There's another kind of heart. A heart that makes people feel uncomfortable in their sin. People who praise and worship God's holiness

feel welcome. People who hunger and thirst for righteousness yearn to be around hearts like this. It's soothing to those who love God. This heart doesn't know much about the latest TV shows and celebrity gossip (yes, gossip), but this heart could tell you so much about the love of God, the wisdom of God, and the beauty of God. This heart knows more Bible verses than music lyrics. It's a heart that has been tainted by the world, but desires purification and is willing to do whatever it takes to be cleansed of the stains. This heart shuns the world and welcomes Jesus Christ.

It's not that the world doesn't want to dwell in this heart, it just can't for long. Every time the world tries to creep in, it gets pushed aside for Christ. This heart is too pure for the world. People living in sin are attracted to this heart and often desire God in this heart's presence, but some people living in sin cannot bear the brightness of this heart, so they run to the prior heart, the heart that makes them feel comfortable. This heart makes sin run. It would tear up if a movie happened to use the Lord's name in vain. It would rather fill itself with things that are pure, things that Jesus loves. Things He died to restore. This heart suffers many lost relationships, persecution, and ridicule. It's a humble heart, though. And through humility this heart experiences true and lasting pleasure and fulfillment. It's not momentary and doesn't depend on circumstances. Sometimes this heart gets the worst "lot" in life, but it would never know because it's too concerned with serving others. This heart is lacking the world, but it has gained Jesus Christ. You can tempt this heart all you want, with any pleasure of the world, any status, popularity, or entertainment, but this heart would rather stay the way it is … filled with Jesus Christ.

What kind of heart do you have? Do you fill your heart with things that are pure and lovely? Things that Jesus would cling to? Or do you fill your heart with things that Jesus would mourn? Who resides in your heart? The world? Or Jesus Christ? Maybe it's a little of Jesus and a lot of the world, maybe it's a little of the world and a lot of Jesus. Either way, our ultimate desire should be to have a heart that pleases Christ. A heart that He would happily reside in. Not a heart that is filled with things He died to cleanse.

Ashley Weis

"Pure and undefiled religion before God and the Father is this: to visit orphans and widows in their trouble, and to keep oneself unspotted from the world." –James 1:27

Stop Telling Me I'm Beautiful

A while back I heard a 10-year-old girl say that her mother is ugly because she has wrinkles. Her mother is beautiful even as she ages. This crippled me. Little girls are basing beauty on superficial things at such young ages. It's no wonder they grow up to be women who need their pictures to be touched up and smoothed out before showing them to the world. I wasn't like that when I was a kid, but I still wanted to be beautiful. Didn't you? I wanted my father to tell me I was pretty and I wanted a boyfriend, desperately, since the age of 9.

I can't believe where God has brought me. I went through a lot. He used George's porn struggle to strip my intense insecurities. When George and I were walking toward healing I questioned myself a lot, asking God to search my heart and show me the truth.

Why? Why does his struggle with lust affect me so much?

I always asked that question. Over and over. Then, I searched through my childhood, teen years, and early adulthood, realizing that my insecurities were growing since way before George came along. It wasn't his porn struggle that made me feel not good enough. Knowing he looked at other women isn't what made me feel like I'd never be beautiful enough to him. It was my own life and the way I let people affect me from childhood and on.

I spent my life allowing people to determine my worth, my beauty. And no wonder George's struggle with lust crushed me to the core. When I married him I believed he would be the one to finally make me feel good enough. He would never treat me like others did. He'd never, ever make me feel not beautiful in his eyes. And because he would always treat me perfectly and validate my beauty, I would spend my life feeling confident and beautiful. Finally.

Beyond the Mirror

But that didn't happen. And I'm glad it didn't. Because I have finally been able to let go of what the world thinks and learn what God thinks of me. It's been an uphill climb and I've had to toss a lot of things out of my backpack to get to the point I am now. It was too heavy to carry and God helped me rid a few things. I stopped wearing makeup, knowing that it was a mask I used, an idol. It was tough at first, but now I feel so much more beautiful without it. I can't even believe I feel that way. I also spent more time with God, learning about inner beauty and a character that shines of Jesus. Learning more about inner beauty has made me want to be like this world less and less. I still struggle sometimes, but I no longer want the kind of beauty this world seeks. I want the kind of beauty that lasts for eternity, not just a lifetime or a few years of dieting and running and never having kids.

I have changed so much, but I had to be willing. And it wasn't easy. At all. Stripping these insecurities from our lives means getting rid of masks. And masks help us hide our flaws, our insecurities. It may hurt to rip the mask off, but life without it will be so much better that you'll never want to put it back on. I want that kind of freedom for all of you. And you can find that whether your husband looks at porn or has stopped, because it does not depend on anyone's view of you except God's.

I can honestly say that I'm at a point in my life where I don't want to hear those words anymore. *You are so beautiful.* I only want to hear them if they are in reference to God's beauty. I'm so tired of myself. I want to focus on HIM.

I don't want to be focused on my clothes, my hairstyle, my makeup, my purse, my shoes, my outfit for so-and-so's wedding—I want to be focused on God and I want deep, inner beauty to grow in me from Him being the center of my life.

Isn't that more beautiful? To be a woman not concerned with what the world thinks? To be confident even wearing a hospital gown? To have one pair of shoes and give the money that could be spent on other shoes to the poor? To be more concerned with the beauty of someone's wedding then what she is going to wear to it? To think more about others than herself? To not be concerned with the beauty this world is obsessed with, but to instead be obsessed with the beauty of God?

That's what I want. I don't know about you. But I want to become more and more of that woman. The woman who loves. Who laughs. Who lives. And who does all of those things no matter what anyone thinks of her. She has no need for acceptance and she never wonders about not being good enough. She's too wrapped up in God and loving others to even think about such things.

I really, really, really want to have that kind of beauty. The kind of beauty that is more concerned with her appearance to God than the world.

Pure in Heart

"We need to skip silver linings and cut right through the clouds to the sunshine. Instead of looking for joys amidst sufferings, we must learn to be joyful amidst sufferings without any reason (silver lining) except Christ Himself. He is our sunshine in dark times. When people hurt us it shouldn't tear us to pieces, because He's all we need. These times of darkness, of suffering, of trials, they are necessary for spiritual growth. And for that reason we rejoice. But even more than that ... we rejoice because each trial we not only endure but embrace with full joy, is another moment in this life we are able to die to ourselves and live for Christ."

— Taken from *Resurrection: Discovering the Beauty of Marriage in the Cross*

A big part of my healing was that I had to learn to see my suffering as something to embrace, instead of something to get rid of in the blink of an eye. The suffering is what changed me ... when I stopped running.

I sort of liken it to a fire. Fires hurt, right? Of course. No one wants to be burned. But we need to be. In this world we are so accustomed to creating these "false selves." We create a version of us, a version we want to be, but it's not who we are. So we try to live up to this false version of us, our false self, for our entire lives. We don't even know who we are anymore. So, God takes us through the fire. He allows us to be burned because He loves us too much to see our true selves weighed down by lies and masks.

It hurts IMMENSELY. But as each layer is burned off another layer of our masks will turn to ashes. Over time, it hurts less and less. Until finally, every layer is burned away and there it is ... your true self, underneath all the layers, it's so absolutely blindingly beautiful and bright and humble that the flames cannot even match it. The flames aren't hot to burn you anymore. And your true self, that beautiful self underneath the layers of masks, becomes its own flame. It is so bright and powerful that the beauty of your own flame will then work to burn the layers off other people. And so on and so on.

It's horribly painful. Horribly. You literally have to die to yourself. Old Ashley was horribly bitter, insecure, impatient, negative, self-centered, and not exactly the most enjoyable person to be around. Old Ashley fades as I stand in the fire, as uncomfortable as it is, and allow God's light to burn off my masks.

I'm still burning.

Those negative thoughts you dwell on may always plague you, but you don't have to give into them. Just as a man who is recovering from lust must take his thoughts captive to Christ, so must you. Every instance you want to dwell on an image of a woman (covetousness) or a thought of what he did to you (self-centeredness and self-pity), give the thought to Christ, tell the thought it has no place in your mind, and worship God with all that you are, leaving no room for lies.

The more layers you burn off, the less these things will even come to your mind. You'll be concerned with other things so much more that you just won't think about it. But for now, it takes dedication, perseverance, and faithfulness. You have to stop these thoughts when they come up, instead of dwelling in them. It's so easy to dwell and be in a state of self-pity, but it's going to kill you. Instead of conversing and consenting to negative thoughts, keep the away from your mind and heart. When you are tempted, flee.

You must embrace the pain and allow yourself to go through the flames. God is teaching to not rely on your beauty. Your reliance on physical beauty is one of the many layers keeping you from being you who are. It's keeping your flame dim. He wants you to look at Him and worship His beauty. It's only through His beauty that any of us are beautiful anyway. Seek His beauty and allow your flame to grow bright.

Ashley Weis

God Isn't a Genie in a Bottle

So many people we talk to expect that God is going to heal them simply because they ask. He is going to rid all forms of lust from their eyes and hearts in an instant, just like that. He is going to heal our hearts and marriages in the blink of an eye, simply because we asked. But God isn't a genie in a bottle. He isn't up there ready to give us our three wishes and move on to the next person. He isn't there to give us the winning lottery tickets or the most dashing spouses in the world.

He is God. He loves us too much to always give us our way. What kind of parent would I be if I gave my children everything they wanted? If I let them drink chocolate milk all day long, have jelly beans for every meal, and never corrected them when they were wrong? What kind of children would I raise if my parenting methods were purely based on granting the wishes of my children?

Probably would raise a bunch of anarchists. God is God. Not a genie. He allowed Job to suffer (didn't cause the suffering, just allowed it) for the benefit of Job and the glory of God. We shouldn't expect anything from God. Instead, we should be so focused on loving Him that we never even give thought to what we can get out of it. It's love for the sake of loving our Father, not love because our Father gives us blessings.

Healing from this comes when we are willing to accept the pain for what it is. We need to take responsibility for our part in this. We need humility. We need to be thankful for pain because it helps us to grow. Pain, if we let it, can strip our pride and help us see that God is all we need. Or, we can choose to focus on ourselves and become bitter. But we need to be thankful for the current pain we are in and know that God loves us and He is only allowing us to go through this in order to teach us something valuable. We have to be willing to learn and grow. Change has to be in our vocabulary if we want to experience growth and the restoration of our marriages.

You stop looking at porn not because God waves His magic wand, but because you hate sin and you take the necessary steps (out of love for

Beyond the Mirror

God and others) to rid this thing from your life. You stop focusing on your insecurities not because God waves His magic wand, but because you hate sin and you take the necessary steps (out of love for God and others) to rid this thing from your life.

Love for God is what will transform your lives and marriages. Not a magic wand.

Pure in Heart and Mind

Purity isn't just for our husband's. It's for us too. We have been trained into viewing the world and ourselves through a tainted mind. And our tainted mind stains our heart. Maybe this is why the end of the verse on pure religion (James 1:27) tells us to keep ourselves unstained from the world. It's difficult to see ourselves, our marriages, our husband's, our children, and even God, through pure eyes when our mind and heart are tainted.

The masks we wear are part of the splattered mess inside of us. But it's more than our masks.

What You Put In, Comes Out

George always says to me, "Garbage in, garbage out." One of the biggest factors in the cleansing of porn from his mind was to "be careful little eyes what you see, be careful little ears what you hear, be careful little feet where you go." This is the same for me in my struggle with insecurity.

If I am constantly filling my mind with People magazine, Facebook updates and pictures, celebrity gossip, movies that blaspheme the name of Jesus and are filled with sensuality, TV shows that reveal the world's views instead of God's, the latest fashion trends, music that screams of impurity, etc. etc. etc. If I focus on these things, these things will taint my heart and mind, and the things that come out of my heart and mind will reflect these things, not God.

I should, however, be filling my mind with "whatever things are true, whatever things are noble, whatever things are just, whatever things are pure, whatever things are lovely, whatever things are of good report, if there is any virtue and if there is anything praiseworthy—meditate on these

things." Taken from Philippians 4:8. In real life this would look something like this:

Instead of focusing on the things in the left column, we'd focus on the things in the right:

People magazine	The Holy Scripture
Facebook updates and pictures	Pictures of orphans who need a home
Celebrity gossip	Stories and lives of great Christian examples
Movies with Jesus' name in vain	Movies that praise Jesus (very few)
TV shows with the world's views	Edifying conversation with family and friends
The latest fashion trends	Clothing ourselves with Christ
Music that screams of impurity	Music that glorifies God

To be stripped down is to be humble. To take the world out of your mind and heart and replace it with Jesus Christ. It seems unnatural to do so at times. We've been so trained into being like the world that letting go of the world hurts. It feels like dying. And there is a part of us that will cling to the world instead of letting go, because we don't know who we would be underneath the layers of masks. We fear the real us. It's too real. Too unaccepted by the world. Too flawed.

Peter tells us to "be clothed with humility, for 'God resists the proud,

But gives grace to the humble.'" That sounds pretty harsh. God resists the proud. How can we truly heal if we are still caught up in the world and our pride?

Insecurities are wounded pride. It is a form of pride that people feel sorry for, but it is pride nonetheless. The answer to insecurities is to focus on God's holiness and to allow humility to enter our lives. First, we need to be stripped until we are clean. Then, we need to stop resisting humility. By resisting humility we resist God's work in our lives.

I think James sums this up well in James 4:1-8:

> *Where do wars and fights come from among you? Do they not come from your desires for pleasure that war in your members?*
>
> *You lust and do not have.*
>
> *You murder and covet and cannot obtain.*
>
> *You fight and war.*
>
> *Yet you do not have because you do not ask.*
>
> *You ask and do not receive, because you ask amiss, that you may spend it on your pleasures.*
>
> *Adulterers and adulteresses! Do you not know that friendship with the world is enmity with God? Whoever therefore wants to be a friend of the world makes himself an enemy of God. Or do you think that the Scripture says in vain, "The Spirit who dwells in us yearns jealously"?*
>
> *But He gives more grace. Therefore He says:*
>   *"God resists the proud,*
>   *But gives grace to the humble."*

Therefore submit to God. Resist the devil and he will flee from you. Draw near to God and He will draw near to you. Cleanse your hands, you sinners; and purify your hearts, you double-minded. Lament and mourn and weep! Let your laughter be turned to mourning and your joy to gloom. Humble yourselves in the sight of the Lord, and He will lift you up.

If you ask me, this seems pretty serious. God resists the proud, but gives grace to the humble. If you resist the devil (pride), he will flee from you. If you embrace the devil (and pride like the devil did), God will resist you. Yikes. However, if you draw near to God, He will draw near to you. We are told to cleanse ourselves, purify our hearts, and humble ourselves in order to be lifted up.

We expect God to heal our insecurities, but we don't expect anything from ourselves. We want our pride to be filled and we fear humility. Jesus was a perfect example of humility. He was God, but treated as though He was a pile of dirt. He didn't exalt Himself. When He was belittled and ridiculed during His final hours, He didn't boast or jump down from the cross to show the world He was the Savior. He didn't flaunt His looks or try to look better than He was created to be. He didn't hide in a corner because He felt sorry for Himself. He lived for the Father with all humility.

Desiring Humility

Our insecurities vanish when we stop seeking pride and start desiring humility. When we would rather be thought of as nothing to the world, than something amazing and beautiful. Humility isn't concerned with its appearance to the world; it's concerned with God and everything through God.

In Matthew 10:39 Jesus says, "He who finds his life will lose it, and he who loses his life for My sake will find it." How much of our lives are we willing to lose for His sake if we can't even forfeit a movie that uses His name in vain?

Beyond the Mirror

And if we aren't willing to lose our lives, how will we ever find life? Freedom from insecurities will not come if we continue holding onto pride. We will only attain what our hearts desire. If our hearts desire to be exalted on earth, we may find that momentary pleasure, but we will lose true life. If our hearts desire to be humbled on earth, we may lose worldly pleasure, but we will find true life.

What is your goal in this life? Is it eternal or temporal? Are you more concerned with watching a movie that misuses Jesus' name than bowing at the name of Jesus? Are you more concerned with looking good to your husband, than *being* good to your husband? Are you more concerned with being thought well of, than proclaiming the beauty of God's holiness? Do you hide your weaknesses, instead of being honest and showing the world that God is strong and we are weak?

Are we willing to say what Paul said in 1 Corinthians 12:9-10: *I will rather boast in my infirmities, that the power of Christ may rest upon me. Therefore I take pleasure in infirmities, in reproaches, in needs, in persecutions, in distresses, for Christ's sake. For when I am weak, then I am strong.*

Are we willing to take pleasure in our weaknesses and distresses?

To desire and love God's will is to know that every weakness, every trial, every hard time in life, is for the good of those He loves. If we trust and love His will, then how can we not love trials? Because trials make us more like Him and less like the world. If we are consumed with God than no earthly sorrow can take away our joy. Our joy is in His will. And we know that God's will is beyond our understanding. If we trust Him, we let go of our fears and insecurities and fall into His undying love.

That is our only safe place.

The Stages of Sin

When George's porn struggle surfaced in our marriage I honestly believed I was the victim and he was the horrible person in our marriage. I believed I was without sin in this particular area and he wasn't. I thought of myself as better than him. Now, I am still not the most intelligent person in the world, but I'm not stupid enough to believe that lie anymore. My insecurities were just as much of a sin (pride) as George's pride led him to lust and use women for his own self-pleasure. Insecurity is a desire for the self-pleasure it lacks in being validated from the world (our husband's). Lust is a desire for the self-pleasure that comes from objectifying people made in the image of God. Both desire something for self, not for God's glory.

That being said, we ladies are not free of sin in this area. We are sinners, too. And our insecurities will not vanish until we take responsibility for our pride (or wounded pride) and work to rid these things from our lives. Let's look into sin a little deeper.

There are five stages of sin. Assault, Converse, Consent, Captivity, and finally Passion/Obsession.

Assault

An assault is a temptation to sin. It can come in the form of many negative thoughts or images. For a man recovering from a porn addiction, he may be assaulted by images of his past as he is trying to get rid of them. He isn't sinning. He's being tempted to sin. We cannot stop temptations and assaults from entering our path.

For me, as I struggled to heal from George's porn mess, I struggled with the following assaults:

- I am not good enough
- God doesn't exist
- She looks better than me
- I wonder what he saw in the grocery store
- He doesn't love me
- I want to have an affair and show him how it feels
- I'm not loved
- This isn't fair
- I don't feel like loving him
- My pain is too much to bear
- I give up
- Divorce isn't that big of a deal, lots of Christians do it

I could go on and on. And if we look under the surface of these assaults I experienced, we see that all of them are self-centered and stem from a shade of pride. The devil constantly tried to get me to turn inward in order to turn my face from God. Satan wants me to be like him, to make him proud. I make him proud when I turn from God to focus on myself. He smiles when I want to give up on my marriage. He laughs when I cry. He absolutely adores my self-centeredness. Can't get enough of it.

When I look back at the years George and I spent fighting over this stuff, I can't help but wonder who I made smile more. God or the devil. Did my character reflect the humility of Christ or the pride of the devil?

I know the answer. I followed the father of lies. I took the assaults to the next stage.

Conversing with Negative Thoughts

In the early stages of our healing I didn't know how to NOT converse with these thoughts. They were a part of me and I didn't know how to rip them from my mind. I conversed with them all day and night, even dreamed of George cheating on me. Let me show you a few examples based off of the list I gave you a few minutes ago. I'll show you how these thoughts became conversations.

I am not good enough. Yes, that's right, I'm not good enough. I've never measured up for anyone. No one has ever loved me for who I am, except God, but I need someone in real life to love me for who I am. Will anyone ever love me? Am I going to be miserable my entire life? Yes, yes, I am.

God doesn't exist. How can He exist when I have this much pain and He doesn't do anything to take it away? Where is He? Why won't He just let me die. I just want to die. I hate that God allows me to suffer. Does He really love me? No, no, He can't, because He doesn't exist.

She looks better than me. I bet George looked at her and thought the same thing. He probably wishes my hair looked that nice. I hate him for what he did. Why can't he just love me and only me? Why does he have to see other women? This isn't fair.

I wonder what he saw in the grocery store. I bet he looked at those magazines. I need to go there tomorrow and see exactly what he saw. I wonder what the clerk looked like. I bet he liked her. I bet he wished he could be with her instead of me.

He doesn't love me. How can he love me and look at other women? How could he lie to me? He is such a jerk. I can't stand him. And he's not even that attractive either. He can have porn and I'll just cheat on him.

I want to have an affair and show him how it feels. He doesn't understand my pain. He just wants me to get over it. Fine, I'll get over it. I'll have an affair and show him just how much I'm over it. Maybe then he can be the one crying himself to sleep every night.

Beyond the Mirror

I'm not loved. I'm not worth loving anyway, why should I expect to be loved? If only I could be someone better. If only I could be confident in who I am. I just want to be secure. I hate myself.

This isn't fair. Why do I have to be a woman? Men seem to have it so much easier. I hate what I look like. I hate my personality. I just want to be done in this world and die. If suicide didn't hurt and I could be guaranteed heaven, I'd do it right now.

I don't feel like loving him. He doesn't deserve my love. He's so self-centered. He doesn't even try to romance me after all he's done. I can't stand the thought of being close to him right now.

As we can see, an assault can easily turn into a conversation. And those conversations generally led me to one place. Pride. And that pride led me to one of two places during that time. Anger or despair. The devil snickered as I allowed some of these conversations to move into the next stage.

Consenting to Sin

At this stage we have yet to commit a sin in action, but we have done so in our minds. There were times I allowed those conversations to keep going until I finally gave in to the temptation. It could have been any number of things. Going to the store and dwelling on images I thought George lusted over, then blaming him for something he didn't do. Murdering him with my words. There were moments when I gave into the idea of cheating on him. Although I never committed this in action, I did so in my mind. I took my wedding rings off and gave up on our marriage.

There are so many times that I consented to these conversations with negative thoughts. So many. And our marriage suffered because of it. As George tried to recover, I drowned our marriage in poisonous thoughts. And for men who don't try to change, women often drown themselves in poisonous thoughts as both husband and wife contribute to the downfall of

the marriage.

The more we entertain these thoughts, the more they come. And as they keep badgering us, we eventually consent to them. And consenting to them repeatedly leads us to the next stage.

Held Captive

Many of us not only struggle with negative thoughts about our marriage, we also entertain negative thoughts of ourselves to the point that we are held captive by them. We believe we are ugly, so we make it a point to strive for the pride of feeling good about ourselves in the eyes of the world (and our own tainted eyes). This stage of captivity can be anything from having an affair to shopping for clothes to fulfill emptiness in our souls.

We can spend hours in front of the mirror and never be satisfied, because we have created a habit of conversing with negative thoughts about ourselves. These thoughts are not our own. They come from the devil. We say, "I'm so ugly," and think it's our own words, but it's not. It's the devil, we simply consent to his words and form negative habits that lead us to captivity.

We are in chains. There is no freedom here. Only darkness and despair. The mirror will never tell us that we're the fairest of all. It will point out our flaws time and time again. We will try on fifteen outfits before we go out of the house, and still not feel satisfied. We'll either decide to stay home and sulk, or we'll go out and buy a new outfit to make us feel better, or we'll put on something that makes us look "horrible" and miserably enter the world.

Chains. Captivity. A dark place that leads us to obsession.

Passions and Obsessions

At this point we've handed the keys of our heart to the devil. We've said to him, "Have your way with me. I'm lost." Sometimes we even enjoy this state so much that we don't even realize we are suffering. Passions and obsessions can often feel good. Porn addiction, gambling, being wanted for our looks, obsessing over material possessions—all of these things can feel good for a little while, so good that we become too attached to even desire

God. We would rather have our passions than have God.

This is why sin separates us from God. Not because God hates us. It separates us from Him because we choose the world over Him. We would rather gain our life on earth and lose it in heaven, than lose it on earth and gain it in heaven. We would rather enjoy our passions than enjoy Him.

And we pay for it. We pay for it with despair, anxiety, fear, insecurity, loneliness, emptiness, constant striving for unattainable things, coldness, apathy, anger, and ultimately, separation from our Creator.

But even when we're entrenched in our passions … we are not without hope.

Fighting Temptations

When negative thoughts enter our minds we should ignore them. We shouldn't converse with them at all. At some point maybe we will be strong enough to fight these thoughts with the truth and scripture, but right now, when we're super sensitive and weak, we should ignore them.

They will only stir dissension in our hearts and minds. They will make us angry, insecure, and annoyed. Self-focused and not God-focused. This goes with everything. When I have a thought like, "Oh, I'd really like to turn some heads," I push the thought away and don't even listen to it. Even when I have a thought like, "I don't want George to see me take a shower because of what I look like," I push it away without giving it a chance to grow roots in my mind.

When you have any thought that is not of God, push it away and focus on Him entirely. This is a discipline. A tough one. Because you are constantly assaulted with these thoughts. Constantly. And it seems to get worse when you try to ignore them. Just focus on God entirely. The more you wrap yourself up in Him the easier it is to love through pain.

Getting Close to God

Every good and bad thing in life is there for us to move closer to God, the question is, will we allow it to be used for that purpose? It's not necessarily that we should desire suffering (because it really does produce virtue if we let it), but we should be thankful when it comes because we know it's stripping us of our issues, our masks, our worldly concerns.

When you say or think you are ugly, you are essentially saying that Jesus is ugly. We are created in the image of God, the image of God being

Jesus Christ—God in flesh and bone. God as human. Every time you call yourself ugly, turn around and tell Jesus He is ugly and not good enough physically. If you can't tell Him that, then look at yourself through Him and realize that you shouldn't call yourself that either.

Ugliness is neither here nor there. Physical beauty is molded according to the culture and highly overrated. We're all beautiful in form, whether the world thinks so or not. The world isn't looking through the right lens. Everything is subjective. To God, culture, fashions, trends—they don't matter. You are you. He created you, to think less of yourself is slapping God in the face.

For me, I needed to stop thinking of myself in order to get these thoughts out of my mind and heart. It is so damaging to focus so much on ourselves and worldly concerns. It will crush our spirit.

The stages of sin that I mentioned before begin with a thought or realization or something in your path. Get rid of it immediately, not by focusing on the thought, but by turning your face toward God. Don't give it anymore room in your heart or you'll end up lost and depressed, swimming against the current and drowning in your negative thoughts. Just think of Him. Look to Him. Be immersed in HIM and all that He is. The temptations get louder as you pull away from them, but the best tool for fighting them is to not even acknowledge them, to just focus on God all the time so that temptations are not even noticed.

Getting closer to God will push you further from insecurity and fear. We are so trained into believing that self-esteem is needed, but this couldn't be further from the truth.

Christ-Esteem is Needed

If your skin was flawless you wouldn't be able to relate to Jesus who was not attractive to the world in appearance. *He had no beauty or majesty to attract us to him, nothing in his appearance that we should desire him.* From Isaiah 53:2.

So why do we elevate ourselves above God's "painting" which is us in our natural state? Jesus was content to not look pleasing to the world's eye, why aren't we? Do we only want to follow Him when it's comfortable and follow the world when Jesus' road gets too tough?

Temptations to be insecure will come and go for you. For all of us. It's what we do when they come that counts. Don't slap God in the face with repulsive thoughts, unless you are prepared to look Jesus in the face and tell Him He is repulsive, then make Him go on a diet and get some plastic surgery so His face is more attractive to Hollywood. Look at yourself through His eyes, dear one, it's the only answer.

To move away from focusing on self and building our egos and to move toward God and building our faith—that is the real answer.

The Son in Your Eyes

Jesus is Better than Vodka

We have a bar near us. I see the same man passionately walk to the bar every day, sometimes very early. He's obviously passionate about alcohol. I don't want an alcoholic to be more passionate about alcohol than I am about Jesus Christ.

Do I get up with the same passion as that man to spend time with my Lord? Do I drink down the Living Water with the same desire and passion as an alcoholic drinks whiskey? Alcoholism starts off with just one drink, but soon ... you "need" another drink. You don't feel like you can survive without that drink, so you always, always drink.

Am I drinking of Christ with the same passion?

I want to.

I want so, so much more of Him and so, so much less of me. I don't want to care about what I look like, dress like, or what others think of me. I don't want to decorate my house while others need it more than I do. I don't want to spend money on clothing for myself when someone else needs it more than I do. I don't want to be so concerned with myself. I want to be so concerned with others that I totally forget to be concerned about myself.

I don't want to be concerned with myself.

I want to live for Him, for others. I want to live poorly (even if we have the money one day not to), so that others may live better lives. It's so hard for me to spend money on new clothing when people in Africa are dying from lack of clean water. Who am I that I should live better than they?

Oh, Lord ... let it be so. Let me be poor so that others can have more. Let me die to myself, to this world, to be closer to You.

It's tough for me to balance some things. It's tough for me to know when to be extreme and when to find temperance. But one thing is for sure ... I never want temperance when it comes to being more like Him. I never want temperance when it comes to following Him and loving Him and others through Him. I want MORE passion than an alcoholic has for alcohol ... and for any Christian who doesn't have more passion for Christ than an alcoholic has for alcohol ... shame on us. Shame.

Jesus Christ is so much better than vodka, so much more life-giving. Let's drink of Him. Passionately.

All for Him

To please my King every second of every day of my life ... that should be my greatest desire. Not to be the most beautiful woman in the world. Not to have better body parts and hair. Not to change myself in order to be accepted by the world. I should desire God more than I desire anything else. That same passion that caused me to cry myself to sleep over George's porn addiction ... I should have as much passion for God. Crying myself to sleep (good tears) over His indescribable beauty.

We should seek holiness with every part of us and desire to live a life that glorifies God in all things, not because we want to be amazing saints, but because we love God.

If there is anything I want to allow my extreme personality to plunge into with all it's got ... it's this. Glorifying God in everything. In the little things and big things. In washing the dishes and watching movies.

Are my actions glorifying Him? Is my life glorifying Him? Are my minute-by-minute thoughts and words glorifying Him?

Let's fill our lives with things that point us toward Him, that make us love Him more. Let's desire to make every minute of our lives glorify all that He is. We should want to seek holiness, to be cleansed every day. We should want to choose good over evil more and more. Those negative thoughts that plague us? We need to hate them and want them gone before we can kill them and replace them with more thoughts of Him and His love.

I want more of our Father, more of Jesus, more of the Holy Spirit in my life. And I know that I have to be the one to choose that. I do have a free will. I can choose to lock Him out of areas of my life. He knows everything about me, every hidden area, but I can still choose to lock Him out. I can choose myself, the world, my desires and passions, and people over Him.

I don't want to choose anything over Him. I want to take the keys from the devil, get rid of all the passions and obsessions in my life that hold me in chains, and find the freedom in giving Jesus the keys to every area of my heart.

1 Corinthians 10:31 says, "Whether you eat or drink or whatever you do, do it all for the glory of God." Yes. That is what I want. To "do it all" for the glory of my Lord.

Before the Throne

Imagine if we lived every part of our lives as though we were literally standing (or kneeling) before the throne of God. I wonder, how different would my life look if I remembered this every second of every day?

Would I lose my patience with my kids at the throne of God? Would I get agitated with my husband at the throne of God? Would I cuss? Would I talk negatively about a person (including myself)? Or would I do everything in reverence and honor for Him?

We often forget that He sees everything we do. We don't always live with an eternal perspective, realizing that one day we will be accountable for every word and action in our lives. We complain about our bodies and our husbands and expect God (and others) to pity us because we are insecure. We all have our pasts. We've all been hurt in many ways. All of these things have added to our current pain. Being molested, used, misunderstood, ridiculed, unloved, treated as an object, and on and on. These things mold our insecurity into a bomb and whenever someone hits a little trigger the entire thing explodes into depression. How is this living before the throne of God?

I want to love Him and worship Him in everything I do. Sex, entertainment, child-rearing, relationships, fun, laughter, writing—I want it to all be something that would have Him say, "Well done, good and faithful servant."

Lord, help me to live my entire life at Your feet, with an eternal perspective that never fades. Help me to love You more, to live through You more. I can't wait until the day I am with You, able to worship You for eternity in my true home. Oh, let it be so. Let it be so.

It's Not About Me

George and I watched a recording that my dad made us of the History Channel's special on the Shroud of Turin. During the documentary, I couldn't stop thinking about all of the blood and marks they found on Jesus' body. I've always known He went through a lot, but that made it more real to me. Then, the next day, we listened to a worship song in the car. I thought of His love even more.

Oh, Jesus. I love Him so much.

I thought about how much I love Him. And how I don't feel like it's ever enough. I've often prayed for a bigger heart simply to be able to love Him more. But then I looked at my husband and realized ... I can love Him more.

I can love Him more by loving others more.

There are so many negative thoughts that run through my head every day. Ugh, that waiter was horrible. Ugh, George is going to kill us in this car. Ugh, the kids are driving me craaazy. Ugh, that person talks too much.

I don't want so much negativity running through my brain. I want to see the world through His eyes—through the eyes of Beauty. I want to love more. Everyone. I never want to take for granted a second with my husband or my kids or anyone who crosses my path. I want to see beauty in the rain, blessings in the fire. I don't want to complain or gossip or speak negatively about anyone.

I want to love Jesus more. I want to value His name so much that I never watch another movie that uses His name in vain again. I want to value His heart so much that I never take for granted what He did for me. I want to value His truth so much that I don't set up my own standards and

Beyond the Mirror

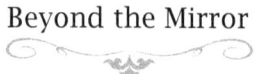

expectations, but live through Him and for Him. I want more of Him in my life. And I want to see it overflow into my love for everyone else.

My husband. I love him. But when I think of him right now as my heart is swelling with love for Jesus ... I love him even more, in a way I can't explain. It's deeper, it's brighter, it's less about me and my feelings and more about the beauty of the person I married.

My kids. I love them. But when I look at them right now as my veins are pumping with this overwhelming love for Jesus ... I love them even more. It's not about me. My feelings. My emotions. My love. My heart. It's not about me. It's about Him—loving Him and letting that overflow into the lives of everyone around me.

Be Your Own God

I know everything. I don't need help from anyone. You can't trust anyone, so you have to rely on yourself. That's what I do. I rely on myself and no one else. I believe I am the best person in the world. No one is better than me. I don't need to stamp God's name on everything I do, I am a big girl. I can take responsibility for my own actions, whether they are good or bad. And most of the time they are good, because I don't have God breathing down my neck and telling me otherwise. I am free. I am living. I have peace and no one can tell me otherwise. It's inside of me. You can find it, too... if you give up God and search within yourself.

Besides, if I were a "Christian"—what is a Christian, anyway?—I wouldn't know anything. I'd only know what I think I know through my own perception of God and Jesus. I can't really know anything. And sin? What right do I have to tell someone else they are sinning? Christian or not, I can't do that. It's not my place to know what's right and wrong for other people, you know? That's just wrong and judgmental. Plus it'll just push people away from "Jesus." What people really need is love. Forget God and Jesus, they just need love. And maybe if we all had this love we'd be able to get over all of our issues with depression and everything. Christian religions just depress people because no one can live up to anyone's expectations and everyone judges everyone. Why would anyone want to be a part of that?

The two paragraphs above are things people have said to me over time. And these people were even Christians, at least some of them. But they say the same things. And it basically revolves around this: You can never know absolute truth or absolute right and wrong.

So, you make your own. You live based off your own strength without God, which will eventually crumble. Even if you last your lifetime pretending, when you die and stand before Jesus...you will crumble.

Beyond the Mirror

But I've talked to some Christians who end up living just like the world because they don't know what truth is and they don't think they ever can. They would be bashed by other Christians or non-Christians for believing in absolute right and wrongs, so they shut up and follow the world. It's just easier that way. It's easier to be admired by the world than to stand up against it.

I want to offer some encouragement to those of you struggling with this. I want you to know that there is one thing that is more important than what the world thinks of you and that is: what does God think of your life? your actions? your heart?

We can spend our life trying to please the world and the ideals we create for ourselves based off insecurity, but we will end up crushed by someone better. There will always be someone we think is better than us. We'll always be running around trying and striving to be better. We'll subconsciously (or consciously) rate ourselves and compare ourselves to others. And it will get tiring.

When we live for God we find rest in who He created us to be. We don't strive to be good; we become better by the love of Him inside of us. He's not a mean dictator that tells us what to do. No, he lets us choose right or wrong. He lets us decide whether we'd rather follow Him today, or the world. Sometimes we choose Him, sometimes we don't. And this is where grace comes in. And I don't know about you, but the more grace I receive, the more I realize what Jesus did on that cross for me, and I fall in love with Him even more. Not because of what He did, but because I can't help it when I realize who and what He is. And the more I love Him, the more I choose Him over the world. When I fail, my guilt shouldn't push me away from Him, instead it should push me TO Him.

The "right and wrong" in this world is to protect us and help us live the best lives we possibly can … for our souls. Living in a world where we all decide what is right and wrong to us, without even thinking about God or letting Him steer our ships, we will create chaos disguised by psychological love.

Ashley Weis

Real love isn't about ignoring reality to let people find "happiness." Real love is only given through Jesus Christ. And that love crushes individual right and wrong philosophies and stands up for absolute truth.

People can make fun of the words Jesus said (I am the way, the truth, and the life), but they are the truest words our hearts will ever hear. They are the words that comfort me when people claim that there is no right and wrong, when they say that Christians are judgmental for claiming they know the only way, the only truth.

With faith in Jesus Christ you can re-write the top paragraphs to say this:

I don't need to know everything. I want to grow and learn from others, to never think I've got everything under control myself. You can't always trust people, so sometimes you have to rely on Jesus. That's what I do. I rely on Jesus and no one else, not even myself because I know that sometimes I've made horrible decisions for my life that hurt me and others. I believe I am a nice person, but I need the grace of God to saturate my life. Everyone is better than me. I am the chief of all sinners.

I don't need to stamp God's name on everything I do and I can take responsibility for my own actions, whether they are good or bad. Because I know that His grace in my life starts with ME choosing to let Him in or keep Him out. I am free. I am living. I have peace and no one can tell me otherwise. It's in Jesus Christ.

I am a Christian—a follower of Jesus Christ. He is the way, the truth, and the life. And through Him, through my union with HIM and not my own knowledge of good and evil, I can know what is right and wrong. And sin? I don't want the people I love to live in sin, because I know what that does to their souls. I don't want to pretend like everything they do is okay if it's hurting their soul.

It's not my place to judge if others are right or wrong, you know? But through my relationship with God, I can see right and wrong. It's not wrong to see sin, but it is wrong to base someone's worth or value off of their actions. It's not judgmental to see a book with a bad cover, but it is judgmental not to pick it up.

Beyond the Mirror

Truth may push people away from Jesus, but if they are going to come to Him they cannot deny truth, because He is truth.

What people really need is love. The love of Jesus Christ. That love doesn't promise a life free of anguish or trials. Some Christian (and even non-Christian) religions just depress people because no one can live up to anyone's expectations and everyone judges everyone. Why would anyone want to be a part of that? Instead of living bound by rules, I want to live in His truth. I want to know absolute truth, right and wrong, and live in the beauty of Jesus Christ.

Ultimately, we have three choices. Be your own god, let the world be your god, or let Jesus Christ show you the way to a God who loves you more than you will ever love yourself.

Love Letters to Jesus

When sorrow climbs up and whispers in my ear,
Let the beauty of Jesus be seen in me.

When anger and hate fight for a breath,
Let the beauty of Jesus be seen in me.

When dreams are broken and loving is rough,
Let the beauty of Jesus be seen in me.

When sin asks me to defend myself and take another bite,
Let the beauty of Jesus be seen in me.

When materialism and sensuality beg me for attention,
Let the beauty of Jesus be seen in me.

When I don't want to change because I'm too comfortable,
Let the beauty of Jesus be seen in me.

When I don't want to love because I fear the pain,
Let the beauty of Jesus be seen in me.

When I can't forgive because I'm tired and empty,
Let the beauty of Jesus be seen in me.

Beyond the Mirror

When I'm kicked and scoffed, bruised and pierced,
Let the beauty of Jesus be seen in me.

When I'm handed a life of thorns when I wanted jewels,
Let the beauty of Jesus be seen in me.

When suffering is unbearable and death is near,
Let the beauty of Jesus be seen in me.

When I walk through the world, amidst its traps,
Let the beauty of Jesus be seen in me.

When the world thinks I'm nothing and hates all I am,
Let the beauty of Jesus be seen in me.

Give Me Jesus

Jesus, when I want to defend my passions, my desires, my sin, or myself help me turn to You instead. When I want to climb in bed and forget about the pain I've caused someone, help me turn to You instead. When I want to walk away from someone because they have hurt me and don't "deserve" my love, help me love them through You instead. When I want to lock my sins in the closet and never expose them to the world, help me turn to You. When I feel like no one understands and never will, help me turn to You, the only one who will always understand.

When I spend my money unwisely, help me turn to You. When I want to justify my sin because I want the world to think I'm perfect, help me turn to You. When I'm tempted to choose anything over you, help me turn to You.

When I turn on the television or watch a movie, may it be pleasing to You. When I talk with my friends or family, may it be pleasing to You even if it makes someone shudder and hate me. When I spend time on the Internet, may it glorify all that You are and not myself or anything else.

Ashley Weis

I want to be a light. I want to be like You. I want to spend my life in Your will, even if that leads me to death of self. I want the selfishness gone—the annoying idea that life is about me or that I deserve anything. I want the pride gone—the part of me that wants to be liked by the world and fears negative comments directed toward myself. I want the idols gone, from my children to my passions—I want to be so in love with You that nothing else could ever match your significance in my life. I want to live a life abandoned to You—not in fear of financial difficulty or difficult circumstances. I want to go, I want to stay—I want to do whatever You want me to do.

I want to be so in love with You that the world could hate me, and I'd have all I need. Happiness could be forever fleeting and I'd have a secure joy in You. Dreams could daily be broken and I'd rejoice in You. Life could be taken, but I'd know that it's only the beginning, because of You.

Because of You I am able, I am freed, I am going home one day.

Because of You...

Because of Your blood red drops on my soul, I am white as snow.
I cannot say enough Hallelujahs to that. Praise you, Jesus. Praise you. You are my King. I love You.

Amen five thousand times.

Lead Me to the Rock

My dearest Jesus, my one greatest desire is to love You more. To be near You in all things. If I do anything in this life, I want it to be for You. If I take one step, I want to step for You. Whether that step is through fire or alongside still waters, I want it to be for You.

When my heart beats for the world, I want it to be for You. Not my own desire to serve, be needed, or love. I want to do, live, and love, for You, my Lord.

At your feet, I sit in wonder. Your words are sweeter than the smile of my babies. Twenty-four hours in a day, you give. How often I waste just one second on selfish thoughts or desires. Every second of every day I want to be wrapped up in You. Even when I sleep, dear Jesus, I want to dream of You.

Nothing is sweeter, nothing is more dear to my heart, than You alone. You are my Abba and my brother, my King and my Savior. There is none like You. There never will be.

You sacrifice and love. You are faithful, just, and true. Your mercy overflows into my life, reminding me how unworthy I am of such a beautiful God. I am unworthy of Your sacrifice, and how much more beautiful that makes it.

I fail You. I am unfaithful. I am selfish and disobedient and unwilling. But You died for me.

Wow.

Jesus, seep into my heart, clear out the rotted and stale parts, the parts that are like the world, and fill my heart with You. I want to be more like You. I want to love like You when I am unloved. I want to step out in faith when I am afraid. I want to do the unthinkable.

How beautiful that as You died on the cross You cried out for God to forgive Your enemies. Your love for sinners is beautiful. More beautiful than I can imagine or describe. Through Your suffering, You thought of us. You thought of those who were spitting on You, laughing and mocking You, and asked that God would forgive them, they didn't know what they were doing.

Jesus, my friend, I want to live like You, to love like You, to be set apart and follow You through life's best and life's worst. My fallible heart is weak, but in You I am strong.

Thank You for dying for me. Thank You for living for me. Thank You for thinking of me and desiring my time when I desire other things. Thank You for being an example of love, sacrifice, and truth. For proving me wrong and making me realize how much I need You.

Why do I ever think I can live this life on my own? Without You? Your guidance, Your heart, Your hand?

Sometimes when You lift the burden and hand me the easy yoke, I feel bad. I don't want to put my burdens on You. I don't want to take the easy

road. But then I realize You are in Heaven now. When You lift my burdens they are lifted and they do not weigh You down. You were already weighed down when You walked this earth with a cross on Your back, blood dripping from your body and mixing with the dirt.

You already carried my burden, my sin, my anxieties and suffering. But You kept Your heart fixed on eternity, on God the Father. You kept Your heart fixed on the purpose of your death. The salvation of people like me. And You died, You suffered, You were poked, prodded, and spit on, gasping for air and enduring the pain of nails being hammered through your flesh and bones, all for me, all for those of us willing to accept the gift.

Oh, how I want to be like You. Willing. Fixed on the eternal and not the temporal. Loving, merciful, empathetic. An outcast to the world, but not to God.

Live in me, reign in me. There isn't a second worth breathing if it is not for You.

In Love with You

Dearest Jesus, teach me about humility that doesn't know it's humble. Help me to be like You, always willing to serve no matter the cost. Cleanse my heart of pride and selfishness. Make me more like You. There is nothing like You.

Show me what it's like to rest in You. To be like a child in the arms of her Father, resting in who she is, in who you made her to be.
Every second of every day...I want to delight in You. Thoughts of You are not enough. I want to know You. I want to be Your friend, Your beloved, Your faithful lamb.

Decrease any part of me that does not live in You. Cleanse my heart, the inside, that the things that come from my mouth and my heart will be pleasing to You.

My days are numbered. Let each one be pleasing to You. In your grace, I want to live every millisecond of every day loving you.

Oh, to worship You in heaven. What a day that will be!

Until then, I am at Your feet, waiting to look up and be blinded by the beauty of You.

His Little Lamb

Dearest King of my life, if only I could love You more, maybe then I could love my husband the way I so desire. And everyone else for that matter. If only I could love You more, love others more, and regard myself or my own feelings less. Lord, my heart yearns for You. There is nothing I want more than to be wrapped up in You, and for You to be wrapped around and weaved throughout my entire life. But I so often turn to myself. I so often desire my own will, my own desires. Your will, Your desires for my life are so uncomfortable sometimes.

But I want You to transform my heart, Jesus. My life ... may it be lived at Your feet, soaking in your Word, breathing in Your life, living in Your love and strength.

I wish I could always sit with You in silence, never distracted by other things. But I desire to glorify You and live through you in those "other things." Help me to glorify You in all things.

Sometimes I look at George and I explode with love for him, but I still don't feel like it's enough. I still feel like I value myself too much. Strip me of these things, Jesus. Strip me of everything that is my self. Fill me, fill me, fill me with You so that I can serve my husband without a thought of myself.

Humble me so that I am not nagging George to be a "better" man, a man I think he should be. Help me to realize that humility for me isn't in making my husband believe my views, but in allowing him to lead our family and trusting that I am in Your hands even when I fall.

Lead me in the way of everlasting life. Sometimes I feel overwhelmed. Sometimes I don't think I can live the life you've called me to. Sometimes, honestly, I don't want to. Oh Lord, it breaks my heart to even admit it, but you know my heart and I cannot hide my thoughts from You.

I am not who I want to be. I do not love as I hope to love, nor live as I

hope to live. My sinful heart so often tries to take the reigns of life, but no matter how much I desire to live a worldly life and seek my own desires, I know somewhere deep inside, somewhere beyond the temptations, there is a greater truth, a greater love, and a greater desire to please You.

You love me. You love me, Lord. What a profound truth. So simple, but so deep and so undeserved. I am your little lamb. In Your arms I want to be, carried by You, embraced by You, loved, so deeply loved, by You. Take care of me, Jesus. Sometimes I am weak, so weak. Sometimes I am unable to think clearly about things. Carry me like your little lamb. Carry me to heights I could never climb on my own. Carry me across impossible waters and through depths in which I'd normally drown.

I don't want to be anywhere else. When my feet are too tired to follow You, when they desire to run off to the world, please carry me. I cannot do anything apart from You.

I am sorry I so often fail You. I am sorry for everything I do that is not pleasing to You. Shepherd, I'm sorry for desiring the world. I'm sorry for valuing myself beyond what You have given me and made me to be. Kind, loving, Shepherd, in Your hands I surrender my life, again, every day.

As difficult as it is to be like You, as displeasing to the world it is to be like You, that is what I desire. Even when my heart is tempted by the world, I pray for the wisdom to seek You instead. When I jump from Your embrace and run off to chase my own desires … Help me, Jesus. Help me to turn around and see that You are chasing me. The world wants me to chase after its lies, but You chase me and only want me to turn to You and allow You to be my Shepherd, my King, my loving Savior.

I am not always the smartest, the wisest, or the best follower of You … which is why I need You. Like your little lamb, I need You to scoop me up and carry me through this life.

I love You. I love You so much, Jesus. And I cannot express how thankful I am to be loved by You, to be Your little lamb. My dearest King, I cannot wait to fall down in front of You and embrace the feet I ache to kiss, the precious feet I long to follow every second of my life.

Beyond the Mirror

There is no better way to live life. Even if it's hard sometimes. Help me to live this truth so clearly. To not hide from suffering.

I want to live for You.

Most Beautiful Me

Dearest King of Kings, so many of us try to "make" ourselves beautiful. We change ourselves to be like someone else. Someone the world tells us to be like. And You love us, You created us, just the way we are. Why do we try to be someone we aren't?

Whether it's something about my personality or looks, there's always something I'm discontent with. I'm not content in You. I try to fill these gaping holes in my life with other things. Books, movies, clothes, and anything but You. I'll always try to fill the holes with something else and something else. Eventually, I'll be so tired and worn out. So depressed. All because I couldn't hand my life over to You.

I don't want to live like that. I want to be content in You and You only. I want to understand my value and worth. And my weaknesses. I want to embrace them, knowing that they glorify the perfection of You. When I mess up, help me to repent and to become more like You. Sometimes I get so distracted, so caught up in trying to be a better ME. When, really, I will be a better me by becoming more like You.

I know some people think that it's a weak trait. But I don't think that's true. I think being like You is being the best me I can possibly be.

I've known people who don't have much of You in their heart, and I've known people who are overflowing Your love into the world. I want to be like the latter. I want to be more like You, Jesus. Those kind of people are beautiful. They are admirable. They aren't leading others astray, to death; they're leading others to the source of life. They are beautiful because they are like You.

I want to be like You. In all things. At all times. Completely content in You. Never, ever this world or anything in it. I want to look beyond the mirror, beyond my own reflection, beyond my heart and my face, and see You. Oh, Lord … let me see You beyond the mirror. Always.

Heart to Heart

Does it Ever Get Better?

The following conversation took place over a span of time. This wife has become an amazing friend through these conversations. We now talk almost every day. Her name has been changed for privacy reasons.

Dear Ashley,

I am not sure where to start ... other than to say thank you for writing on your blog. Thank you for having the courage to talk so openly.

Almost seven years ago I came home from work (I was on staff at a church) to get some information for a research paper I was working on. I couldn't remember the website I had found the information that I needed, so I pulled up the Internet cookies.

My life changed that day. I found several links to pornographic websites. My stomach sank. I knew I hadn't visited those sites ... and there was only one other person that it could have been.

My husband.

I called him at work and simply said, "Have you been looking at pornography on the Internet?"

His responded, "I don't want to talk about this now. I will be home right away."

Within the hour he was home and was standing in our kitchen. He was admitting to his pornography use. We had been married ten years and he had been looking at porn our entire marriage. I was crushed. My response to him was sincere. I said, "sin is sin" and I forgave him. But instead of dealing with this issue then, I stuffed it deep inside. I immediately accepted the fact that I was somehow inadequate and this drove him to porn.

Beyond the Mirror

I lived that lie in my heart, beating myself to pieces for years ... I would scour the Internet to see the girls he looked at, to learn everything I could about porn, or to find help.

Nothing helped.

My husband would say little other than "he was walking away from it completely" but I needed to know details. I needed to know how, why, when ... but we didn't talk about it.

After having this pain fester for years, I finally broke recently. My pain poured out. My husband was (and is) in shock. He had no idea I had so much pain. Yesterday I stood in our kitchen again and told him that he had a heart issue and needed to work it out with the Lord. Like it is my place to judge his heart ... and then after all of these years of searching I came across your website yesterday.

I felt such relief. Someone who knows how I feel! Someone who has been there and isn't afraid to sugar coat the truth. Someone who has said and done some of the same things I have said and done ... and wow, someone who made sense of this mess we are in. I was so convicted by some of the information because it was the missing piece in my healing. I was looking to my husband to fill a void that isn't his to fill. I realized that I have a heart issue ... and that was the very thing I was telling my husband!

God used your message in a mighty way and I want to thank you. In fact, I wish I could hug you! :) My husband is a commercial photographer so there is much that goes with that industry that makes me cringe ... but I have hope that I can heal now ... because for the first time in years God spoke to me and I listened. Thank you. I am also the president of a nonprofit. Funny how I spend my days helping others and I couldn't even help myself ... and I have been so lost in this pain and heartache. Thank you for what you are doing. If you get some time, I do hope you will write me back.

Blessings,
Lauren

Ashley Weis

Dear Lauren,

Thank you so much for your lovely, encouraging email. I was so blessed by your words. I am so glad the blog has helped you in this way. It really, really blesses me to hear that. I pour my heart into it. Thank you so much for sharing your heart with me. I, too, would scour the Internet, his history, even just look at porn to see what he might have seen. Oh, it was horrible! So horrible! I just drowned myself in miserable, negative thoughts, comparing myself to so many women and never feeling like I could measure up to be a good enough wife or woman for my husband.

How is your husband doing now? Is he seeking change and purity? How are you? I know you said that you realized you have a heart issue too ... but how are you feeling now?

Love,
Ashley

Dear Ashley,

WOW - this email means so much to me. THANK YOU! I haven't had a chance to write you back yet and I want to apologize. It's been a tough month. I could definitely use continued prayer for protection of my heart. It seems to break very easily over every little thing my husband does (or doesn't do) and protection over my thought life. I can't quite keep from beating myself up over and over. It's a terrible cycle. I need to break it.

It means so much to me that you took the time to write me back. I hope you can forgive me for taking a month to answer. It's been a tough month emotionally ... and in addition to that, my kids have busy schedules, and moving my office from one town to another.

I ordered Exposed and it arrived today. I am anxious to read it.

My husband seems repentant but I don't think he guards his eyes the way he should ... and I am not always certain that he REALLY understand the depth of my pain. He seems to think I should snap my fingers and be over it. And maybe I should be over it. But I am not ... and it is something I am aggressively trying to deal with. I seem to continue to wrestle with this demon ... over and over over. Does that part EVER get better?

Blessings,
Lauren

Dear Lauren,

Thanks so much for ordering Exposed. Let me know if you like it.

A common problem women email me with is that their husband says he has changed, but they don't see that he looks away from women. I don't think men really do understand the depth of their wife's pain. I always recommend that wives have their husband's read Exposed (if they feel okay about the porn star part) so that he can see just how it makes a woman feel.

A husband recently read it and said it completely changed his life. Here's what he said: *I am finding my heart breaking as I read it. I can't believe how my actions have been so hurtful to my wife, the women I've dated over the years and the women I've objectified. I don't like that part of my life and want to leave those old grave clothes buried.*

Anyway, I wish women could snap their fingers and get over it, but it's way too hard to do that. I think it can happen quicker than it tends to happen (for me it took years), but since I've been talking to so many people I really think it can happen quicker, just with the right mindset and heart-set and a husband who is truly changed and faithful. Of course we can change our hearts even if they don't change, but it just takes longer I think.

It will get better though. The temptations to be insecure will always be there, just like he will always have the devil trying to get him to lust. But the temptations lessen their hold on you. You don't give into them and they just end up ugly to you, instead of something to sink your teeth into. Does that make sense? :)

Love,
Ashley

Ashley Weis

Dear Ashley,

Do you ever feel sad anymore? Or did God completely remove that pain? And how do you do everything you do with three small children? Please know I appreciate all you do -- and the time you have invested to answer my emails is beyond kind. Thanks. :)

Lauren

Hey love,

I never feel sad anymore, but I do feel insecure sometimes. But I went through a huge journey and my insecurities are rare nowadays. I'm just a different person now. I haven't worn makeup in a year and have no desire to anymore. That's saying a lot for me. But yes, God completely removed the pain. Otherwise I wouldn't be able to talk about it so much, it would just be too painful. But we talk about porn and lust almost every day around here! And do everything I do with three kids... Well, I don't. I pretty much never have time for myself. No hobbies. Nothing like that. I am pretty much always cooking, cleaning, working, or taking care of kids. And my house is never, ever clean (at least not every room all at once). So ... I don't really do everything. Haha. I just try to get by one day at a time!

I consider talking with other wives my only hobby. :) So thank YOU for emailing me!

Ashley

Dear Ashley,

I am still reading Exposed ... great book. GREAT BOOK. So very much captures "how it is." I am so very glad you put pen to paper and published this book.

How are YOU? Does anyone ever ask you that? You have such a heart for everyone else. I sometimes wonder about you. Can I pray for you in any specific way?

Lauren

Beyond the Mirror

Lauren,

I'm glad you're enjoying it. :) Let me know what you think when you finish.

I'm doing well. Believe it or not, a few people do ask me that. Haha. You can pray that God would continue to strip the desire for worldly beauty from my heart and that I would be able to serve my family humbly and joyfully in all things.

Thank you, my dear. And please keep in touch with me. :)

How's everything going on your end?

-Ashley-

Ashley,

I've wanted to drop you a note ... just haven't. No good excuse other than I am struggling more than usual lately. It seems like every where I turn there is some kind of reminder that spins my "I am never going to measure up" mentality out of control. I really hate that this ever happened to our marriage. :(

-Lauren

Lovely,

That still happens to me. It's just everywhere, ya know? But thankfully it changes a lot once the marriage heals. Now ... It's an ongoing process for me to lay those prideful desires to be that worldly kind of beautiful aside.

You can measure up if you change what you want to measure up to. :)

How are you doing otherwise? How's hubby?

Ashley

Ashley,

Hubby is good. I don't see anything other than desire to continue to heal our marriage. I am grateful for that. He came to my office and left a note on my car today. I thought that was very sweet. I'm good. The kids keep me busy and work is crazy busy ... I've started teach a 6th grade girls

class at church. I am excited and humbled and hopeful all at the same time. I want to focus on investing in these girls. I so very much want to get where you are with the beauty outlook. I stopped buying magazines ... but am stalled on where to go now. I hate the worlds idea of beautiful ... but then I also worry I don't measure up. I sound deranged, don't I? Oh goodness. :)

Lauren

Lauren,

This is a long one, be prepared. :)

I did a lot of things to get rid of that desire for the world's beauty. I got rid of makeup about a year and a half ago. George loved it.

I wrote another blog post talking about it here:

It's been a few months now since I've worn makeup (minus one day). It's not that I think wearing make-up is "wrong," but since asking God to examine my heart every day lots of sinful habits have been unraveled.

When I felt convicted about wearing makeup I tried to think of every excuse I could. Oh, it's not that bad. It's not like I'm wearing alot, at least it's natural-looking. I don't need to wear make-up, I just enjoy it. I need to look like a woman, and have fun with my femininity. What about my husband? I should look good for him.

The very fact that I didn't want to stop wearing make-up enough to make up 500 excuses told me that I had a problem. It wasn't hard for me to see that my motivation for painting the face God made up was purely vain. My reasons for wearing makeup were:

1.) I didn't feel pretty without it.
2.) I felt like I needed to measure up to the world, the beauty advertised on magazines.
3.) I was insecure.
4.) I wanted to be noticed for my beauty.
5.) Didn't want my husband to think someone else was prettier than me.

Okay, so I could go on and on, but all the motivations are the same. Vanity.

Beyond the Mirror

Insecurity. Acceptance. Approval from the world. Validation from someone/something other than God. I was looking for my value in something other than Jesus. Make-up made me feel better about bags under my eyes after a sleepless night. It added color to my pale winter face. It made me feel better about myself.

Well, God convicted me about this and I couldn't deny it any longer. I couldn't continue wearing makeup knowing that I was doing it purely for the wrong reasons. (I tried to tell myself sometimes that I was doing it for enjoyment and because I love being a woman, but the more I asked God to reveal my sin to me, the more I realized I was lying to myself.)

When I first gave up makeup it was hard. Seriously. I'd be in the shower making up excuses to paint my face. Really, I couldn't help but laugh at the intensity of which I relied on makeup to feel content with my appearance.

It's been months, or weeks, since I've really worn makeup. And you know what? I feel BETTER about myself. George told me I looked pretty today and I believed him. Normally (with a face covered in makeup) I would have shaken my head and disregarded his comment. Today, I believed him.

I no longer rely on makeup to feel beautiful, to feel like the perfectly designed Ashley God fashioned. Now, I accept what HE designed. No longer do I feel the need to accentuate or add to the Me designed by God.

I don't want a need/desire to seek my value/worth in anything other than Jesus. The need to adorn myself to feel beautiful. The need to hear people tell me I'm beautiful in order to feel beautiful. And really, the need/focus on outward beauty in general. I want to find my worth in Jesus. I want to be so focused on Him that the LAST thing I care about is my reflection in the mirror or my appearance to the world.

Then, a few weeks ago I was in bed with my youngest baby ... I have a lot of time to think with her. I get real honest with God because I know I can't hide from Him. I've been struggling lately with desiring humility and feeding my pride. I recognized that I don't really desire humility, just to feed my pride. And the clothing stuff is just like the makeup. My husband thought it was crazy when I first told him I wanted to get rid of all of my clothes and wear one (pride and prejudice regency looking dress) every day of my life. But ... he wants me to pursue holiness. He is very much into having a noble wife and not just an attractive wife. He wants a treasure, not a trophy.

That being said, I'm really struggling with this one. I have been extremely humbled and I can't honestly say I've always desired this humility. I miss being an object of lust. Isn't that horrible? I really miss being noticed for my looks, my clothes, my nice shoes ... It sounds horrible saying that, but I'm being honest. I've gone back and forth the last few days, telling George I can't do this. I want to be beautiful in the world's standards. I want to have nice clothes (I've already gotten rid of them all). I've actually been depressed about this, but I've realized something today as I pondered your email earlier (before I started writing back).

I've realized that when you die to yourself and your old ways ... it's a death. It's okay to mourn a death. And I do. I miss those old ways, but I don't want to. This is a good death. I want to rejoice with this death, because it brings life. So ... as hard as it is to continue on this path, I'm going to. George has seen me swing back and forth with this, and this is a really hard thing to decide, but I think I need to stop giving in to the pressure to be attractive in the world's eyes and just keep this stuff stripped from me.

As for your own heart, allow God to shine lights into the motivations for your actions. If you desire to give up makeup and can't because of a job, question whether your job is worth it. I know that sounds crazy, but if you can't work somewhere without being fake ... ? You know? Of course I have very extreme views on this, so you'll probably never hear another person say this. :) I know I'm weird. Trust me!

As for George's reaction ... he loves this.

Now, as for pushing your hubby for too many answers. What are you asking and more importantly why? That's the real answer. Why are you asking him?

Thanks for letting me spill my heart. You're one of the few people who know all those things.

Love,
Ashley

Love Can Overcome This

The following conversation took place over a span of time. This wife has become my very best friend through these conversations. We talk every day and she is handling her situation with more grace than I could ever imagine. She sacrifices for her husband even when he hurts her. She is truly beautiful. You can read the beginnining of our friendship below. Her name has been changed for privacy reasons.

Hi Ashley!

I'm so excited that you emailed me back so soon! My hubby and I pray together every night for healing for us as individuals and in our marriage. And I always pray for a stronger relationship with Jesus for the both of us! I feel like this is part of an answer to those prayers!!!!!!!!! I found your site by going to bing and searching for blogs for wives with husbands with porn addiction. I've been reading on your site for hours now! Its amazing to find this. Do you write or talk with a lot of couples/spouses?

Well, I'll give you a quick history of us and our issue. Our 2 year wedding anniversary is this month! I've known for a while about his porn addiction and lust addiction. He denied it up and down, even swore on our marriage he doesn't do that while looking me right in the eye. I felt it in my heart for so long. There were times I thought I was crazy and believed him even though I saw his evidence. Finally, I confronted him again he gave in and said yes he's doing it and its an addiction. Since then he says he hasn't looked at porn once and has no desire to ever do it again. His main struggle is lusting with women in general. I just don't believe it, after all the lies before. He always acts like it's under control. Let me add that his job involves computers, so he knows how to hide his trails, yet when he got lazy I caught him. I feel like he's trying to smooth everything over and just hiding it better.

But there are good things he's done. On his lunch break he walks to a church and prays, he started praying with me outloud every night before bed and after a fight. He leads the prayers. We became members of a church and go every Sunday, he listens to podcats on porn recovery and now is starting to leave posts in forums - looking for a man to talk too. Some of these things I know because he just TELLS Me.

Some I know because I'm there with him.

Heres the downfalls, I see him looking at women and he "cant remember doing it" or doesn't even notice that he does it. I see him gawk at magazines at the store. He looked up a girl online at WORK and didn't tell me about it. He had an excuse. He didn't even tell me about that one, I looked at the history and saw it. AND the Real Problem to me....everyday he comes home and says he had a "good day" meaning not lusting over sexy women or billboards. How can one be addicted and always have a good day?? That makes me not trust! And I think I am so vulnerable that I refuse to open my heart to him.

He says that I have a problem and need extra help but he's got it all under control.

Sorry this is lengthy. Thank you for reading.

Congrats on your baby as well, when is your due date? Do you know if you are having a boy or girl?

-Noelle

Dearest Noelle,

Congrats on all of your excitement this month! :) That little baby's birth is going to be so amazing. Can't wait for you to experience that.

It sounds like your husband is taking steps toward healing, which is great and more than most men. It will take time though. He cannot possibly have everything "under control" at this point. I don't know if any of us ever do. These struggles (for both men and women) are lifetime struggles. To say we have it under control is pretty much giving ourselves a greater opportunity to fall later. We can be better every day, and we can have truly changed hearts, but can I as a woman honestly say that I've got my insecurities under control? No. And I don't think a man can say his problem with lust is under control. It's really not about control, it's about laying down our tainted hearts and allowing God to renew them, giving us new, clean hearts and eyes.

The way your husband sees women is impure, but it can change. When he spots an immodest woman he doesn't see an insecure heart in need of love (which is why they dress the way they do), instead he sees "sexy." He sees her as an object. He uses her. This isn't the way God wants men to look at women.

Men will never be able to avoid seeing sensual imagery or immodest women ... But they can change the way they look at these things. First of all, lingering on these images ... Not good. And the only way he can change this is if he does the following things:

1.) Draws closer to God and learns to see women through His eyes.

2.) Cut out his eyes. This means no mall, no grocery store lines, no movies over a PG-rating, no internet without someone around, filters on all computers (x3watch), etc. This sounds crazy to some people. But if he's serious ... He will cut these things out for a little while. Until he can see through pure eyes, he needs to get rid of everything that taints his vision. Know what I mean? George HAD to do this in order to change. He still doesn't frequent the mall, we have no TV, and he is VERY careful about the movies he watches.

When both of these things come together ... Love for God and discipline ... His heart will slowly change. George is a different man now. Of course there are immodest/sensual women and pictures in this world, but the way he sees them has changed. He knows what it is and refuses to give into it. He knows that it's only an image—it has no control over him. He takes every thought captive. He looks away when there may be something that tempts him. And he has truly lost the "desire" to go out and look at stuff. Of course there is still the temptation to look when something pops up, but he doesn't seek it out anymore and he doesn't give in to the temptation because he has new eyes and a new heart.

All of that will take time.

As far as your heart goes ...

First of all, having him come home every day and say it was a "good day." I probably wouldn't buy that either. George had a real problem with lying when I first found out. He wouldn't tell me when he fell or looked at someone lustfully, but I started prying it out of him because it drove me insane. I wish he would've just been honest with me in a natural, healthy way. Eventually he started to open up more (when I stopped freaking out so much). He would tell me things like, "I saw a magazine come into work today and was tempted to look, but didn't." Or he'd say, "I saw such and such billboard today and looked, but I'm getting better." He told me what he went through. I got to see his heart.

I can't say how important that is. You have to be comfortable enough to hear his heart without getting upset and angry. It's okay to be insecure, but be honest. When he tells you what he goes through, tell him from your heart (without anger) how you feel, how insecure it makes you, how you don't feel like you are good enough. Try to hear each other out and learn to understand each other, instead of always trying to get your feelings out. Same with him.

He needs to realize that, yes, you have issues even though he may be getting better. Your trust for him will not be regained until he proves that he is worthy of trust. That takes SO much time. It took us a long time and George did quite a lot to prove that to me. He even made me search for images on the computer when he needed one for design. He wouldn't get the mail just in case something was in there. He really proved himself to me. Over time—over A LOT of time—this helped me to trust him. Now, my heart is in his hands again. Fully. It wasn't during the healing process. It just can't be. Yes, we are to love. Yes, we are to forgive. But like you said

Ashley Weis

... We are vulnerable. We've been hurt, lied to, and treated as though bodies are more important than our marriage. That's not a healthy marriage. So our husband's can't truly have our entire hearts until they choose to give us THEIR entire hearts, which involves cutting out their eyes, drawing close to God, and seeing sex, beauty, and sensuality through God's eyes, not the eyes the world trains them to see through.

As far as porn goes, though ... He may not have a desire to look at it, really. Some men actually look at it and don't want to. It's almost like a natural, impure reaction. They just do it because they have for so many years. It's alluring, tempting, curious. They just wanna see it, even though they know it's wrong and really, deep down, don't desire it. I hope that makes some sense..

Urge him to be honest with you, even when it hurts. And be willing to see into each other's hearts. Also, look into the reality of the porn industry. He needs to understand how much he is hurting himself, you, and the people involved with porn when he looks at it. This stuff is so deep.

Anyway, I'm sorry to hear about your hubby's dad. Cancer is such an ugly thing. I will say a prayer for him and your family.

Our due date is May 29th/June 3rd. They aren't totally sure. Our first is a girl, second boy, this one is another girl. :) Fun, fun times! In fact, my 3-year-old is now screaming bloody murder in her room as I type this. Always lovely. Always. :) ENJOY those baby days. Everything after 2 is insane.

If you ever need someone to talk to on the phone I'm up for that too!
Ashley

Hi Ashley,

How are you? Congrats on your bundle of joy as well! I hope you have a very easy delivery!

Thank you for your reply! I think my husband is making changes, but you are right when you say that as a wife you cannot fully trust him during the healing process. I showed him blogs you and your hubby wrote. He said that emailed your husband. He doesn't understand what is acceptable when it comes to looking at women. Can you look once? Is that lusting? Is it looking twice that makes it lusting? or looking for more than 10 seconds that means your lusting? I think he asked your husband those questions. He knows looking is a natural instinct but when is it wrong? He knows now that you have to look at women the way God looks at us, (from your blogs!) He needs to learn how to do that, I think. Even just yesterday I noticed that he's looking at cleavage and "sexy" women on TV. He's learning though. He didn't tell me about it, but I saw him. The day before that he took me on a date and said that he's really trying, and for some reason this time I believed him! Things have been going pretty well for me because of that.

One other thing he said was that he's the type that has to learn on his own. I've explained things to him about whats acceptable and whats not and why, how it effects me and our marriage. He goes against them, even calling me names at times (he always apologizes later) I feel like saying I told you that before just listen to me! Sometimes I do say that... He has to find his own way, he doesn't listen to me. This makes it hard because my feelings end up getting hurt usually. And I dont want to take control of his recovery!

I told him about my insecurities and he feels so bad that he caused some of them. I truly felt and sometimes still feel ugly because my husband would look at everyone but me!

I'm nervous about summer coming. He'll see these types of women all over. It doesn't matter what I look like but I don't have all of those things he considers ideal. And I'll be just getting over being pregnant. Even if I was the "fantasy girl" (that's hard to hear him say, but I don't freak out, just listen) he'd still look at other women. Honestly, if I was that type of women and he had these addictions, I'd be afraid that he wouldn't really love me anyway. Do you have any advice on how to get through this part? Prayer alone? I'm religious and pray everyday but do you have any key points to

praying? If that makes sense. How do I make him more comfortable to talk?? I just listen but for some reason he's still not ready maybe to talk? He's afraid I'll get mad or upset/depressed. How did you handle this with George?

Thanks Ashley,
Noelle

Dear Ashley,

I hope you get my email. I'm writing right now in a weak moment. My husband printed our what your husband's emailed to him and let me read it. That was really great, he did that on his own. I dont think he still fully understands what needs to be done (cut his eye out) but I pray it comes with time.

He wants more recognition for the progress he's made already. I'm afraid to give it to him, because then he'll think everythings okay with us. He said he's uncomfortable to talk to me, and doesn't want to deal with me or upset me. Thats probably why everyday is a "good day." I dont think he opens up to me enough.

He said he wants privacy about the things he's saying to your husband. Then tells me to tell him every feeling I'm having (so he can make it all okay). So I said it should be open both ways. He freaked out and got mad at me. It makes me feel like he's hiding something from me but I didn't say that to him. He knows that though he can tell. He really reacted quickly to what I said - makes me suspicious.

I feel like what dont I know now?? This is so hard for me, I hid the fact that I cried about it. Normally I let him see my tears. He makes everyday a "good day" and if I seem happy because of that he acts like our marriage is getting back on track. He says "We're back!!" Well I dont think so because he's not comfortable to talk to me, which may be my fault. He said when I'm crabby he doesn't want to deal with me and that I was crabby before pregnancy (I dont think I"m crabby a lot! I think thats some excuse) so he didn't feel comfortable with me before either. That breaks my heart.

Why did I not know that?? I feel like theres so much more going on inside him or hidden that I dont know or didn't know before. I'm scared. I have to pray that God shows me the way. I feel like reading the private email he sent to your husband. Yet, then I'll feel guilty and I'm starting to have labor cramps I think (dr says its going to happen this week). I've been feeling crampy for 2 days and I dont want more stress if I find out something I dont want to know. I can't handle everything right now, when labor comes I can't be worrying about us. I just never thought when we bring our child into the world that we'd be not right inside. Its so hard for me to even kiss him goodnight, I dont want kisses or anything, it hurts too much.

Thanks for reading my vent,
Noelle

Dear Noelle,

I can feel your pain like it's my own.

Your husband needs to tell you everything you want to know. Period. I wanted to know things that probably weren't healthy for me, and George told me. Even though the truth hurt (which it will) I wanted to know and deserved to know. And while it did hurt, it helped me to regain trust because I knew everything. You know? Because porn is such a hidden secret it's so hard to regain trust if the husband isn't willing to tell the wife whatever she wants to know. Some wives only want to know some things, other wives want to know everything. Whatever YOU want is what he should give, with no complaining.

Another woman has been emailing me this week about how uncomfortable the TV makes her feel and that her husband refuses to get rid of it or cable. I don't get it. If a husband truly loves his wife he should be willing to do whatever she wants right now. He should see her

get uncomfortable about the TV and go throw it in the trash immediately, without even being asked!

Your husband can't use your pain as an excuse to withhold the truth from you. That's the entire reason George got so into porn during our marriage. He didn't want to "hurt" me, so he just lied and hid stuff and eventually it piled up.

Your husband needs tell you whatever you want to know. Otherwise he can pretty much except your distrust to grow and your insecurities to increase. I don't know about you, but when I didn't know something I imagined things to be WAY worse than they actually were— which caused major issues.

I can't stress this enough to husbands, but this is what I want to scream to all of them: LOVE YOUR WIFE MORE THAN YOURSELF.

Don't wait to be asked to do something. Don't wait to be asked to stop going to the beach in the dead of summer—just do it. Don't wait to be asked to turn off a Victoria's Secret commercial—just do it. Don't wait to be asked if you were tempted to do something—just tell her. Don't wait to be asked to leave a restaurant if the waitress is skimpy—just do it.

Isn't your wife more important???

I mean, really. What does it take for a guy to realize that he has to do whatever it takes to regain his wife's trust? That he as to LOVE her and seek to understand her no matter what? That he shouldn't wait to be asked to do something like a child, he should be man enough to understand when his wife is upset and bend over backwards to make her feel better. This is, after all, pain caused by HIM.

Okay, now that I got that off my heart. :)

It's okay to feel all the feelings you are feeling. Your husband has to step up and deal with the pain that his sin causes you. Period. It's all difficult to work through, but love can't possible overcome this if he doesn't allow it to. Light has to shine on the dark corners of this. If we keep the light out of certain areas because of our fears ... It will never, ever be illuminated.

BTW — You can always call me if you want.

And also, congrats on the due date approaching soon. I'm getting the cramps too, but I should have another few weeks. I HOPE. I'm not looking forward to that pain again.

-Ashley

Hey Ashley,

My husband and I had a major discussion last night. We ended with deciding to talk to you and George about it. He's kind of hurting inside that I dont come over and show him affection on my own. He's the one that comes to me to give me hugs and kisses and things like that. And I told him that I'm just not ready to do that on my own yet. Sometimes I am, I have my moments.

And even when he kisses me, on the forehead or lips wherever, I want it but at the same time I dont like it and dont want to give kisses back. I'm lonely inside without his affection yet cannot accept it. Then I feel so bad because he said he needs me to show him affection. He needs to be loved by his wife or he'll die inside. He said if it takes too long for me to come around again, bad things can happen to us.

I pried to find out what that means and he finally said divorce or cheating or depression. Then reassures me we'll be together forever and get through this. It's a catch22 he says, because I shouldn't do that if I'm not ready, yet if I don't we're in more trouble. How can not give me as long as I need to heal?

He says he problem is in the past and I need to heal, I Am Trying! And its not in the past because he's still struggling with lust. I dont know how long my healing will take! So we settled on, when I'm having a good moment to just love the heck out of him. When I cried, he says he wants me to be strong, but its okay to cry infront of him. He says I can't handle this stuff.

Ashley Weis

Which makes him want to be all positive and maybe not tell me painfully honest things because it hurts him to see me sad. Am I supposed to hide my feelings inside?? And then he says the pregnancy is making me more emotional, maybe its true but any wife would feel the way I do inside.

Heres the second part of this. He said what is a marriage with out trust? I just gave him a look on that one... come on! He knows I'm nervous with the summer approaching and he thinks that he'll probably be able to handle everything by then. Only God knows he keeps saying (true). He thinks maybe God will give me trust by the summer time - thats next month!

I feel like we have to get through the summer first! And my insecurities come into play here too, I'll just have had the baby and wont be in shape like the women he lusts over. (Also, the ones he lusts over aren't "regular women" like me, which is hard on me again.)

We'll probably be going to the pool a lot this summer with his family. Then this came up ... On Feb 9th was when we had our talk about the porn and he began his changes. That was our big day. He told me that night that when it comes to bachelor parties he'd go to the dinner and come home. He'd be skipping the other "festivities." He will probably be the best man of his brothers bachelor party. So he'll be planning the whole thing and be expected to go. They may get engaged with in the next year. He still says that he wont go the strip clubs but he will go the clubs downtown to have a good time with friends. He said he wont look at any of the women and if they talk to him he'll tell them he's married. He said he wouldn't go unless he's "cured".

I dont think its right that he'd put himself into a situation like that. At those dance clubs all the women dress provocatively, including the bar tenders and there's usually women dancing on platforms in a push up bra, fishnets and thong. Or they have provocatively dressed women dancing on the bars (employees or drunk girls, either!) We've been to those clubs many times, that's how it is in downtown Chicago! Unless you go to a small sports

Beyond the Mirror

bar or something, but even there you'll probably see some women like that on Saturday night!

He says the dance clubs are completely fine and there's women like that everywhere day and night, you cannot avoid it. I think that you shouldn't put yourself into that situation! He says during the day at work there are women walking around. so you'll see it anytime, no need to avoid the night club and be unhappy in life bc you can't hang out with your friends. I disagree.

Let me add this, on Feb 9th he said about just going to the dinner and coming home. Now he said he just meant no strip clubs. He's changing it on me. I asked what if I'm not comfortable with you going? He said he'd go anyway because he wants to be with his friends that one night. He doesn't want to be controlled (I didn't say you can't go, I said you shouldn't go). He said my feelings are too much

He feels it's okay and he'd override how I feel because he thinks it's okay. He also said that I shouldn't go either then to those places, I didn't argue that back though. I asked what about how much you love God and me? Is going to the club for a few hours worth that much to put our marriage through that? He said he'd go anyway!!! He wants to be happy.

So you get the point here. He'd do it anyway regardless of my feelings and everything, he made it clear. I'm too emotional and getting into this too much. I don't think so. He tells me he loves me sooo much (and I know he does..), yet theres obviously restrictions on it. He'd be depressed and upset if he cannot do certain things and go out with friends sometimes because of this lusting addiction. Ashley, I'm hurting inside more than ever right now. That shows me how much he loves me. He said we might end up divorced if I dont fully trust 100% over time. Funny how this switches over to be my problem, not our problem or his, Mine.

Now that your husband is better from his struggles, he wouldn't want to go to a night club with his friends because God would have changed his view on places like that right? That's what I told my husband, that would happen to him. What about a regular small sports bar just to talk in with the guys for a little bit? He still wants to be a normal guy, but changed inside. I think he's worried about his friends rejecting him from participating in the bachelor party night club thing. They dont know about his lust addiction stuff! But he still wants to go too (night clubs not strip clubs), to have fun. I need to say that I have no problem with him hanging out with his friends, I want him to do that once in a while. I just don't want him to go somewhere that is inappropriate for him and go there regardless of how that makes me feel!

Tomorrow we have reservations to go to a nice brunch to celebrate our second wedding anniversary. We said a long time ago we'd privately re say our wedding vows. I dont feel so thrilled about it now --- especially when people say happy anniversary to us ... real happy right now.

Thanks for reading this long one,
I think my husband is gonna email George on this too today.
Talk to you soon,
Noelle

Hey Noelle,

Print my email out and share it with your husband.

First of all, he's not loving you more than himself.

He needs to stop thinking so much about himself. You are the wounded one here. Wounded by his betrayal and unfaithfulness. Yes, you need to love him more than yourself too. You need to stop being selfish and you need to desire to please him (not his lust) more than you care about yourself being pleased.

He needs to stop thinking about his needs and think about yours. I didn't receive love, kisses, hugs, or anything like that from George for about an entire year. I wanted his touch, but at the same time despised it. I wanted him to hold me, yet at the same time despised his touch. I needed his love, but his love reminded me of his unfaithulness. His touch made me think of how many times that same hand masturbated to other women.

So it took a long time for me to truly receive his love and affection. And it took a very long time for me to GIVE it without hesitation. Sometimes I gave it even when I didn't feel it, but that would eventually make things worse.George learned to understand that I needed time (lots of time) to heal and to be able to initiate any kind of intimacy with him. It took me FOREVER to take showers or undress around him again.

Your husband needs to know that this is a time of HIM proving his trust and love, not you. You need to use this time to learn to accept his love again. To receive his kisses as genuine, even when it hurts. But as for initiating? How can you if you don't trust him with your heart? You can't give someone your heart fully unless you know they aren't going to spit on it.

By him telling you that divorce, cheating, or depression can come from your lack of initiation and affection ... He is pretty much setting his marriage up for failure and you for more pain. He has to own up to the pain he caused you, stop thinking about himself, and do whatever it takes to prove his love and affection to you. The last thing on his mind should be himself. If he keeps thinking like that you will never heal or trust him again.

The porn may be in the past. But the problem is not. The problem is right now. The problem is that he lied, cheated, and lusted after other women and his wife is in deep pain. That is your current problem. It's not in the past, and it won't be until he stops trying to fix YOU and instead seeks to LOVE you.

And girl, you are totally normal for not being about to "handle" this stuff. What real, genuine woman can? The women who fake their strength just pretend everything is okay, but inside, this stuff KILLS us. It eats at our very souls. Your husband needs to understand the fact that you are a normal, hurting wife. He needs to understand that this is hurting you and

instead of fearing your pain, he needs to take in every single tear as his own. He needs to realize that all of those tears YOU are crying are nothing compared to the tears God cries over this situation. He wants to see your marriage restored and it can't be if either of you focus on yourselves.

Pregnancy making you more emotional? Not really. I've had much worse days post-pregnancy than I did when I was pregnant.

Also, don't go to the pool. Don't go the beach. This is my opinion and my advice. I just don't think either of you ar ready for that environment. George and I don't go anywhere near beaches or pools and it's been years. I don't think we EVER will. Women half-naked? George would NEVER even consider a beach, even if I wanted to!

And I wouldn't do that.

Also, trusting him by this summer? Not gonna happen, especially if he isn't willing to be open with you yet out of fear of seeing you cry or become upset. It's going to take LOTS OF TIME, maybe years, to rebuild your trust. And he has to be selfless, patient, and willing. If he's not ... your trust meter will go up and down like a rollercoaster.

Now, for the bachelor party. If he's planning it ... he better make some plans to have a pure bachelor party with no clubs involved, otherwise he's asking for your heart to be hurting again.

A downtown club is completely out of the question for a couple in this situation. Of course, this is only my opinion, but that's not even something George or I would do even now. Or before porn. It's just inappropriate on so many levels. Clubs are 100% not an atmosphere for married people who actually want a beautiful marriage. They are made for single people who want a one night stand.

Thankfully, George sought to love me through it all and do whatever it took to make me feel comfortable and trust him. Otherwise ... I truly think our marriage would have deteriorated. So you are a much, much stronger woman than I am. Truly. I think I would've lost my mind by now.

Beyond the Mirror

I can't imagine what you must be going through. Your husband obviously loves you, but he obviously loves himself more. I'm sorry if that offends him, but it's the truth. If you told him to go sit in a pot of boiling water right now he should be willing to do it.

George won't even go near a television. Do you see how I regained trust? Can you see why it didn't take me longer than 2 years to come to a point where I think I have the best marriage in the world? Because my husband truly seeks purity. He doesn't watch sports, because of the commercials. He doesn't go to bars. He doesn't go out with friends unless it's a normal restaurant with no bars or TVS. He refuses to be seated in the bar section of a restaurant because of a TV. He's lost friends over this, been ridiculed, he's been called "whipped," and he's even had his own family tell him that he's lost his mind and is being controlled by his wife.

George does these things because he desires purity for himself. Period. He wants to please God, and by keeping himself from silly situations where lust is so easy, he is able to find that purity and please God in that area. The benefit is that I've seen him change. I feel 100% at ease when he goes to the grocery store because I know he doesn't look at those magazines even when I'm not around. I know it because I see it in his desire to stay away from anything at all that could be dangerous for him.

And because of him ... because he chooses purity over the world ... he chooses me. He chooses me over those other women. And I can trust him again because of that.

If your husband wants you to trust ... he needs to lay his life down. He needs to lay his reputation, his life, his needs, his desires, his fun, his friends, and even his family down. All for God, and for you second.

I seriously hope this gets better for you. What horrible timing!!

Love,

Ashley

Ashley Weis

Noelle,

Checking in! Baby still hanging around inside mommy?

Just wanted to check in with you and let you know that George is planning on emailing your husband back, but he's pretty much going to repeat everything I said to you. :) Also, I wanted to let you know something.

You are beautiful, no matter what anyone thinks. It was so hard for me to get that through my head. I compared myself to women so much and wondered if George thought they looked better.

I want you to remember that you are beautiful no matter what anyone else thinks, including yourself. Don't compare, don't be jealous, just be you. Rest in who you are. Your husband may end up going to these bars and pools. And while it will really break your marriage, don't let it break you. Does that make sense? You can't control him. You can only ask him to love you with the same love you give him. If he chooses that stuff over you ... Let it affect your marriage not your own heart. Don't give him the power to determine your worth or beauty based off the way he treats you. He's just a person. He will never be able to complete you like God and by the sound of his tone with you ... It seems like he is more focused on himself right now and his own needs/desires.

I'm hoping he will change. That he will truly lay his life down for you and realize that HE is the one who caused this and HE should be the one asking what he can do in order to make you feel safe. But if he doesn't ... Remember that you are beautiful. You are loved. And simply because of the beauty you've shown by sticking through this with him (when he is obviously still too focused on himself) ... You have proved that your inner beauty is just as beautiful, if not more, then anything the world could ever see with their eyes. And that's more important.

So rest in who you are. Don't let HIS eyes determine your worth.

Hugs,
Ashley

Beyond the Mirror

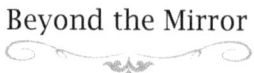

Hi Ashley,

Yes, baby is still hanging around inside Mommy! He must really like it in there! We are going to the Dr today, I'm so curious to see what he says, hoping he does not want to induce just yet.

Today is our actual anniversary. We skipped that brunch yesterday because we were talking all morning long. Saturday night was the hardest night of our marriage and possibly of my life. To hear the words he said, I kept telling him that he didn't realize what he doing to me and what he was saying. He recognized it more on Sunday morning.

Taking a break and getting sleep helped a lot. I explained about laying our lives down for each other. The most impornant thing is giving everything inside of us over to God. Tell him we are weak and we give it all to him, ask for his help, beg and trust that he is going to be there and make us heal (as indiviuals).

I told him to pray harder than he prays for his father to get better (meaning that he has to truly want Gods help that much). I teach him a lot about faith, some things he doesn't know. not saying I know all by any means! I explained that praying like that is when you are on your knees, hit rock bottom and even cry, showing God that we truly need him in our life. He is in our life right now but we obviously are being so selfish that we are ignoring what he would want us to do. (That's my opinion.)

After all that, on Sunday morning we reviewed things. I explained my points in more depth with him and have come to sort of an understanding. It all rests on if he will truly give himself to the Lord. I have to too. I had even mentioned very seriously that we may need a separation now.

I could see the heartbreak in his eyes. I told him how God hates divorce and wants us to have a loving happy christian marriage. My husband is just so afraid of giving up the things he's always loved and feeling unhappy. I told him God will show you happiness and you will not miss certain things. He will open your eyes! I think it takes baby steps with him. To say you can't do this or that, he gets overwhelmed. We prayed together outloud, taking turns as we do every night. This time with such a seriousness to it. There were tears. After we prayed we both said we felt a sense of peace in our hearts. We gave everything over to God! It was a moment. I am so proud of him for trusting in God and also because my husband goes to a church on his lunch break everyday and prays for us, his dad, our little one.

Thank you for emailing me today to see how things are and to let me know I am beautiful no matter what. That is something hard to grasp at times!! I really appreciate your reassurance. I am so sensitive right now. Even some of the things he said the other day still stick in my mind. When it upsets me, I'll just pray and let God know how I'm feeling. God's given me strength to still be here after the words spoken that night. I think a lot of women would have walked right out after some of the things he said.

I just felt like that was not my husband talking, like I didn't know him. For some reason I don't want to give up. I don't want to be a fool either, but God's not going to give up on me and we've come far with other parts of our marriage that I believe we can still overpower this. Now my husband is trying harder and is going to keep praying and having open communication with God. I believe if we both do that we will grow. If he slips with this then he knows we are back to where we were before, talking about a separation.

We sent beautiful anniversary cards to each other today with a lot of meaning in them. I talked to him about how were bieng sweet right now doesn't mean everything is okay. I'm afraid if he thinks its all okay then he'll relax on the seriousness of our situation. He understands that he said. He said he thinks Gods giving us another chance and we don't want to blow it because there might not be another one after that.

Please say a little prayer for us if you don't mind.

Thanks for again for thinking of us. :)

Noelle

Beyond the Mirror

Noelle,

That is beautiful. Really. I love your heart. Love that he seems to be coming around.

Love,
Ashley

Dear Ashley,

I just want to say that finding you and George has helped us a lot in so many ways. It's amazing that you can relate to my feelings when half of the time I thought I was crazy or overly emotional like my husband would say. I thought I was different than other wives but then thought, they've got to feel like me. Now I really see that I am like everyone else!

My husband likes being able to talk to George and he trusts what he says. That's huge for him, for us. You guys are truly a blessing in our lives. I feel like we are making progress even though we are just in the very beginning of healing. Thank you for having your blogs and reaching out to husbands and wives like us. God is working through you to give comfort and direction to us in need. We are so glad to have found you guys! :)

Love,
Noelle

Noelle,

Thank you so much for your sweet words. Baby coming yet??
Love,
Ashley

Hi Ashley,

How are you? Still pregnant? Our little one arrived!! That was his actual It was the most amazing experience of our lives! I ended up having the epidural.

Ashley Weis

Today is my husband's first day back to work. It's a little scary to be on my own. My mom's coming over today for a while to clean and cook for us! I get worried about him going back now that it's really warm out around here ... you know, the women thing. We've prayed a lot about it. I have to keep trusting in God to help me get through this! I feel like I'm here at home and he's out there in the world with all the women..ahh.

We had a incident when we got to the hospital. I was getting checked to see if I was leaking amniotic fluid (I was!) and I thought/noticed he was checking out the cute nurse. Then she retook my bloodpressure and she commented on how it went up. What a coincidence? I dont think so! When she left the room we talked about it. He can't recall checking her out. Then later he said he was looking at her tag bc she had pictures of her kids on there. It fell right in the middle of her chest .. she was wearing baggy scrubs so its not like it was super attractive he says. He said he sees how that might seem like he was checking her out. I noticed he was looking even when she was turned away from us. That was not the right way to start off labor but we got back on track. I had to!

Then I was looking at a magazine after he had and there were ads in there that I found inappropriate. He couldn't recall them and was getting really mad at me about it. He even said some stupid stuff like if you're not gonna start to heal then we should get a divorce! He said I'm doing great and you're not recognizing anything that I do! Then he went through the magazine and said "is this bad? is that?" I got so upset I was crying.

It was hell. We were both sleep deprived and stressed. Once again we made up. I don't know where the magazine went. I dont know if he threw it out, or took it to work with him. I can't find it.

He said he was going to send George an email soon. I'm not asking him if he sent it because I want him to do it on his own. As of right now we're doing good. How did you handle that first summer after your pregnancy? With all your hormones and everything. I'm gonna keep on praying that

Beyond the Mirror

God comforts me and is with my husband. I keep breaking down about him going back to work and leaving me here. I hate the fact that he can look anytime anywhere. Being sleep deprived makes it worse!

Ok well I wrote you a book here!

I hope to hear that you had your little one soon! I can't wait to hear your baby story!

Love,
Noelle

Dearest Noelle,

Your baby boy is so beautiful! I'm past my due date and no baby yet. :) So glad everything is okay and your labor went well, minus the emotional stuff you went through. I told George how he went through the magazine pointing out stuff. Noelle, that is so horrible. I can't imagine what you must have been going through. It doesn't sound like your husband is very sensitive to your heart or needs.

George received an email from him, but would really prefer to talk to him on the phone if your husband is up for that. If not, he can email him but it may take some time. We are really busy and George has been in and out of here getting so much done. But he would love to talk on the phone.

I think you are completely justified in your lack of trust. I don't think your husband has done much to make you feel safe or like he cares about you more than himself. He really needs to stop being so selfish and realize that his problem is still a problem for YOU, even if he "thinks" it isn't for him. He needs a major heart change, like all men do through this. You do too, but the safety and beauty of your marriage largely depends on his attitude right now, which isn't healthy. If he mentions the word divorce one more time!!!! That word should never be mentioned, much less during or after the labor of your first child!!

Ashley Weis

Hang in there. Don't worry about him looking at other women, okay? That's his problem if he does that, not yours. You need to realize that you are beautiful and stop comparing YOURSELF to other women. Stop feeling like you need to be "sexy" to be beautiful and work on your heart, being a beautiful mother, and a gentle wife. You really need to develop a security in your beauty that is not dependant on your husband. But at the same time, if he wants your marriage to survive, he seriously needs to do whatever it takes to rebuild your trust.

My insecurities have greatly diminished since George first told me everything, but if he wouldn't have worked at rebuilding my trust I would have been "healed" but our marriage wouldn't have been healed. You know? Those are separate. Your heart needs to heal without his help, but your marriage ... your marriage cannot heal if he continues to act like this and put himself first. He has to do WHATEVER you ask and know that when you trust him more you won't be as crazy. :) I made George drive down random roads just to avoid billboards in the very beginning ... now, things are a lot different.

Hang in the there, love. Enjoy this time with your baby! It goes so fast! And let us know if you want George to talk to your husband via phone.

Love,
Ashley

Hey Ashley!

I wonder if you've had the baby yet? It can be any time! I can't wait to hear about it! Send me some pictures when your ready too! I'd love to see them!

I think I need to focus more on healing by myself instead of worrying about what he's doing. Like you said. It's easier said than done for me, but I have to because otherwise I'll go crazy. I think I have a little already. I realize that I make it more about what he's doing and forget to work on myself. Thank you for bringing that up in your email! As for my husband, I'm up and down in emotions over him.

He does things that makes me feel more secure, ex. the other day he went into a Catholic book store and bought a marriage prayer that fits our situation and now were saying it together everyday. He did that all on his own. He says he'll do anything to take care of us and fix us. He says he's got God with him and he's working on the looking problem so it goes away completely.

When he does things like that I feel better and think maybe I'm just not healing and what if he really is? But then he says stupid stuff sometimes that brings me back to my sad untrusting state. What if I am wrong in feeling so untrustworthy and am missing out on his changes?? So many things go through my mind. I just keep praying that God leads me on the right path.

When I told him that George wants to talk to him on the phone he was completely up for that. So that makes me feel a little more secure too. But like I said, when he says something like divorce or get so mad at me for being sensitve I go right back to before. Or when I see him looking, I go right back to before. I know he still has to work on that so its going to still happen but it hurts to see it! Overall I'm in the untrusting saddened state of mind most of the days.

So like I said my husband is up to talking to George. So however you want to coordinate that we will. I'll check to see if you write back soon!

Love,
Noelle

Dear Noelle,

We had our baby. Little girl. I'll write more later. :) Everything still okay on your end?

Ashley

Ashley Weis

Hi Ashley,

Things are going pretty good lately! We're loving our little one and doing pretty well with the lust/porn stuff. I realized something since I wrote to you last. I said in my last email that I need to focus less on what my husband is doing/thinking and more on myself.

Well I want to change that to focus more on God. Why didn't I realize that before? I knew it but maybe didn't GET IT as much then. I see my husband focusing more on Him and keep thinking I need to do that too.

I didn't know how and maybe still don't fully, sounds stupid (I thought we had a good relationship all my life, I pray everyday) but I'm still trying to let go and let Him take over this for me.

I've felt like he's not hearing my prayers and I read one of your blogs that said if you're feeling like that maybe your pushing Him away. I think I'm afraid to trust Him ... how can I be afraid of God?? This is crazy but it's the truth! Then I pray for forgiveness over that! Maybe this is Him starting to work a change in me, since I realized this. I'm still hesitant because I'm scared but I know at same time He wants to be there for me. Did you ever feel like that?

My husband told me that he had a breakthrough yesterday. He saw a provocatively dressed woman and immediately like an instinct thought to himself that it was bad. And said a prayer right away. He said for it to be a quick reflex and to not want to look again was new and he was proud of himself. Do you think that's God working in him? It's still hard for me to hear that story even though its positive. It must be my jealousy still hanging around, this will all take time for me to get through.

How are you guys all doing? How is your little girl?? I bet she's amazing! Can you send me some pictures? How are the other kids with her? What's her name? How was labor? Tell me all about it! :) Are you nursing? I hope your getting as much sleep as you can! :)

Noelle

Beyond the Mirror

Noelle,

I've been having a rough time. Getting mastitis five-hundred times. Never had this before with my other babies. Other than that things are going well though. Glad things are going well with you. I hope you're still hanging in there and looking toward the light and hope. Hopefully God has been working on your heart and insecurity. That jealousy and insecurity can ruin your marriage as much as his lust.

I just don't linger on those thoughts even though they come up. It's tough. So many insecurities. It's hard to grow passed them. God has taken me far, but it's still tough. I know you'll continue growing too. You are really working on getting your heart right, I can tell.

Here's a pic of Gwen.

I did get your email with the baby pics. So adorable. Looks like a perfect, healthy baby. So tiny and cute!

Keep me posted on everything!!!

Ashley

Hi Ashley,

My husband and I just read Georges response to his email. We have had a looong weekend. We skipped out on the entire weekend starting on Friday night, to talk through all our issues. It became a marital 911. We never hit a low like this one before.

How did we get here? Everything built up, including the baby taking all our time and us getting no sleep. It's like we come from different worlds. So as you know from reading my husband' email, and I admit, I am hyper hyper hyper sensitive. (I'm so glad you can relate to me Ashley.) I know me being like this is making matters worse! It's like I cannot help it, I let it consume me!

I want to change so bad but am SO afraid to open my heart to my husband again. We need a new system … when he gets home from leaving the house for any reason he gives me the account of if he had seen anyone. This is making it harder on me than better. He used to say everyday was a "good day."

How could that be when one has addiction? How do I know how he has handling things without asking? By actions? But I still see him look at women in public and then he says, "Yes, I saw them, but didn't think sexual thoughts about her."

I just dont buy it. He remembers how shes built or how in shape she is … so to me he's checking her out. How do we update eachother on this without the daily accounts?

He had an "incident" while going down the stairs on the train and this woman was coming up the stairs. The lighting was dim and it reminded him of being at the strip club. But right after he prayed. He said that he did not lust because he didn't have lingering thoughts about her. But since it was such a temptation was that lust? If so, it's ok because I dont expect perfection from him, just honesty.

Let me say that I did not know the details of this situation until we talked this weekend. He orginially said he saw a provactive woman. Now I learned about how it was so intense … what gives?? I want honesty from the beginning!

Another time I emailed you was about the movies situation. He does not want to give up movies, "his passion," because the content makes me uncomfortable. He says that its unfair for me to take that away from him.

If it makes me uncomfortable, be willing to forgo the movie (even if its the one he wants to see soooo bad) because my feelings are more important! He argues it! He says down the line I will be less sensitve and we can watch movies with a quick topless scene in it and it will be no big deal for him (because he'll be cured,and for me). I doubt it! I say if you are changed by Christ then you wont want to see movies with sexual content. So heres the question. He wants to compromise. He doesn't want to see the women, just the movie, what if we skip through the sexual part and just watch it? I dont know how I feel about that. This is a big argument for us.

I need to not freak everytime we leave the house, it will kill me if I let it. We have not gone to church since the baby has been born because its been so crazy right now. I know we need to go again. Do u have any prayer suggestions for us?

Thanks for checking in on me,
Noelle

My lovely, lovely Noelle,

I was probably even crazier than you are. Trust me.

I'm going to be completely honest with you and I may say things you don't want to hear right now, but I would have wanted someone to be honest with me.

I'm going to start with your husband though. And please show him my email. He needs to read this too. Your marriage is seriously on the rocks right now. And you have two places you can go from the lowest point: up or divorce. You can either choose hope right now, or you guys are going to head for disaster. You don't want that. I don't want that. Your baby doesn't want that. You need to choose hope and healing and it's not going to be easy.

Your husband needs to let go of his own desires. This isn't just about porn anymore. He needs to do this in every area of life. He's too selfish. Sorry to be so honest and he may not want to hear those words, but they are true. He's too focused on his own needs and desires, on his own fun. I'm not even going to get into what I think about movies in general, but I just want to say that any movie with sexual content should not be something you let into your hearts, especially right now. I don't care how "good" the movie is. I just want to ask your husband, "What's more important to you? Your wife, your marriage, or movies?" Any man who chooses a movie over his wife's feelings is extremely selfish and needs to question his true devotion to her. This is not something to take lightly. It's not just a movie. This is the heart of a hurting wife we are talking about here. Why are we playing games with it? Why are we wanting to fast-forward through that stuff? That's not going to help. You still catch glimpses of things when you do that. And by the way ... You can judge all content of a movie on Pluggedinonline.com before watching it.

George is serious about this stuff. He doesn't watch any movie with the slightest hint of anything sexual in it. And that's why our marriage is better. That's why I trust him again. That's why he is such a changed man. He allowed God to change him, instead of resisting and making excuses for movies and stupid stuff of this world that means NOTHING when we die. We need to be more focused on things that matter AFTER we die even while we are on this earth.

Noelle, I completely agree with you that your husband needs to be honest about those "incidents" from the very start. If you want him to tell you things like that he should call you immediately and give you any detail you want.

But ... Now ... We need to address your heart. You are extremely insecure. You care too much about what you look like to others and to yourself. You set expectations for yourself that are not something God would smile upon. You are too focused on the external.

These things are contributing to your hyper-sensitivity. You need to realize that it doesn't matter what people think of you. It doesn't matter what you think of you when you look at yourself through the eyes of this world. Stop doing that. Learn to see yourself through God's eyes and stop caring what people think. Stop basing your worth and beauty on what your husband sees. Even if you had a husband who was unwilling to change in this area (that would be extremely sad and make for a tough marriage) you could still heal in your own heart. You could believe you are beautiful. And you can stop comparing yourself to other women. Most of the time men lust and do not compare their wives to those women. WE do that. Women do that constantly, even before we get married. Before your husband came into your life you were comparing yourself to other women. His sin has only made this increase in your life. Now you are trying to compare yourself to women that his eyes see AND women you see. It's making you go nuts because you feel like you need to know exactly what every woman he sees looks like, just so you can compare yourself. And what does that do?

It doesn't do anything positive, that's for sure. It makes you feel worse about yourself and it makes him feel like a little boy controlled by his mother. Not healthy for a marriage. Not healthy for your own heart.

Hope this wasn't too harsh. But I really believe you guys can find hope. It's all a matter of being willing to let go of the things that are ruining your marriage. Lust and insecurity together are deadly. As you are experiencing now. Don't let it kill your love. Remember why you said those vows in the first place. Love CAN overcome this, and it WILL ... If you choose it.

Love ya guys,
Ashley

Our New Beginning

This is yet another conversation I've had over email. All of these women have become my friends. This is the last one I'll share. Her name has been changed for privacy reasons.

Ashley,

Thank you so much for writing this blog. I just found it after a terrible night between my husband and I. What can I do? I feel like all hope is lost. I don't know who I am, who he is, what our marriage is and if it was ever real. I feel so lost. Your site has helped so much, but I'm just wondering if there is anything else you could say that would help. I'm so hurt right now I can't even see straight.

Thanks,
Dana

Hey love,

I know how you feel. There were so many nights I felt like that. Who did I marry? The man I married loved me, treated me with love. This man ... does he even love me at all? It's so hard. So many lies have covered your marriage for so many years that it's tough to know what is the truth.

Lust is huge. It's a huge problem for so many men. I doubt there is a man on earth who hasn't dealt with this to some degree. That thought alone used to kill me. I figured I'd rather be single than married, because all men are pigs. But all men are not pigs. We cannot possibly say that we (women) are not pigs (because we sin constantly as well) and claim that men are because they have problems with lust and purity. It's not easy in this world.

Beyond the Mirror

So many women I talk to complain that their husband's have issues with lust, but they are the same women who hide their flaws behind makeup. How can we expect our husband's to love natural beauty if we ourselves are giving in to the cycle? Lust is deeper than pornography. It's lusting after something that isn't real. And we feed this desire with our current culture. We push makeup, fashion, and outward beauty, even in Christian circles. It's no wonder we are all insecure and struggling with lust. We promote lust all the time, even if it's subtle.

I know that you are hurting so much right now. But I'd urge you to step outside of your own pain and think about this entire world. Think about the pain porn stars are going through. The idea of selling your body to be loved, to be good enough, and never knowing that God loves you. Look at the big picture and realize that you are a sinner, too. Not just your husband. You can't dwell on his sin and sit in your self-pity. It'll just break you to pieces until there is nothing left of you to give to the world.

Allow God's love to pour into your life and overflow into this world. This would needs more sacrificial love, it has enough artificial beauty to last centuries. Let's focus on love.

Hugs,
Ashley

Dear Ashley,

Thank you for your email. I have to admit, I didn't want to hear that at first. I wanted someone to relate to me and tell me that it's okay to sit in my self-pity, but you are telling me to get out of it.

That seems impossible sometimes. How do I ever stop focusing on this stuff? How do I ever feel beautfiul to my husband and feel like our marriage is okay? Sometimes I wish he'd just cheat and leave so I could find someone else who will love me better.

So sad still,
Dana

Ashley Weis

Dearest Dana,

I completely understand. When someone hurts us our natural reaction is to protect ourselves. To feel better about ourselves, even at the expense of the other person. We want to be the victim when our husband's cheat, because fact is, we are the victim in this. But we aren't the only victim. That's they key. Your husband is a victim too. A victim of lies and lust.

We need to fight the desire to protect ourselves and instead we need to desire to protect others. To love others more than we love ourselves. To not run from our husband's because they don't love us the way we think they should. We need to love them anyway. Unconditional love.

You will only feel beautiful to your husband again if you stop trying to please his lust, and instead please the part of him that yearns for purity and God. You shouldn't strive to please his lust, because you will fail. Lust is never pleased. It wants everything and everyone at all times. Purity wants God and everything through God. Be beautiful to God and you will beautiful to a part of your husband that is hidden right now.

Love him through God's love. Don't try to do it on your own terms. Just love God more, and through that love, you will love your husband more no matter how he treats you.

It's easy to want to run from pain. It's easy to want to leave your husband and find someone else who will love you "better." But no man can love you like Jesus. Stop running from pain and run to Jesus. And when you are in His arms, ask for the strength to face pain and love others even when they hurt you. We need to stop running from pain and into the arms of divorce. Men are not the answer. God is. He is the only one who can validate your worth and beauty.

Focus on the beauty and character of God, and less on yourself. Over time, your beauty will far surpass the eyes of lust.

Love,
Ashley

Beyond the Mirror

Dear Ashley,

    It's been a while since I've written back. I just wanted to let you know that I put what you said into practice and you would be amazed at the results. My husband was changing before I emailed you, but I never believed him. I always gave him the worst looks, always disgusted by him even when he wanted purity. It was just so hard for me to deal with everything and like you said ... I think I wanted to stay the victim because it made me feel better. Well, after your email I thought and prayed a lot and realized I needed to love my husband no matter what he did to me.

    I started actively loving him with all that I had and it was amazing. In only a few short days I saw major changes in him. He started to pursue me more and planned romantic evenings without me having to ask. I have to admit, it wasn't easy for me to be romantic in those times, but I pressed forward and loved him through it.

    We have had an amazing few weeks. I've been reading your blog like there's no tomorrow and my husband has been reading it too. I've seen him change sooo much and I am too. It's absolutely amazing.

    I can't say that it's just me for loving him. I know it's God. Wow. I'm still in awe.

    Thank you for pulling me out of the pain and telling me to love beyond myself and to reach for God and not the world or my husband. It has made so much of a difference to stop focusing on myself and to focus on God. I've been more able to love my husband and in turn, he is doing things for me (he actually got rid of the TV!) without me asking.

    Our marriage is so much better and I know this is only the beginning. It's our new beginning like spring after a long winter. I'm so excited, Ashley. I can't thank you enough. If you are ever in the area, please stop by. I would love to give you a hug. I will keep you posted about our progress. I still have insecurities to deal with, but I've been learning to see God instead of myself and it's made all the difference.

    Thank you, thank you, thank you!
Dana

EXPOSED

Allyson Graham, marriage counselor and lover of love, lived a life of romance few could imagine. Until her husband's secret addiction stared at her from the computer screen. Will she be able to forgive the man who lied to her all of those precious years?

Follow her painful story alongside the heartbreaking story of Taylor Adams, a young girl searching for her worth in the world. As Allyson struggles to forgive her husband for lying about his addiction, Taylor naively falls into the same self-destructive industry and discovers that the attention and fun is nothing like she thought it would be.

Purchase at Amazon.com and Barnes and Noble stores

RESURRECTION
Discovering the Beauty of Marriage in the Cross

George and Ashley Weis have endured the flames of porn in their marriage and come out on the other side. Now they want to help you find a way out of the fire. In this workbook they travel with couples through three sections. *Looking Inward* dives into a short journey of the past. *Looking Upward* takes couples through a study of the Beatitudes of Jesus and how they apply to our marriages. And *Looking Outward* courses the ways we can love each other through the mess lust creates in our lives. Your marriage can experience the beauty after rain, but you have to be willing to take the steps to get there. It's not easy, but it's worth it.

Purchase Online at Amazon and Barnes and Noble

Read more at morethandesire.com

www.ingramcontent.com/pod-product-compliance
Lightning Source LLC
LaVergne TN
LVHW041334080426
835512LV00006B/444